THI   ᴄᴀᴇᴅ

VOL. II

HIS DOMINION

"His dominion shall be . . .

Unto the world's end"

By

Charlotte M. Mason

Public Domain
Charlotte M. Mason
Original Publication Date: 1908

This book is Part Two in a multi-volume set
of poetry covering the life of Christ.

Reprinted June 2015

Minor alterations have been made to the content by the
current Publisher for clarity, and the painting reproductions in
the original were left out of this edition.

————

ISBN-13: 978-1514370544
ISBN-10: 1514370549

THE SAVIOUR OF THE WORLD

VOL. II

HIS DOMINION

CONTENTS

INTRODUCTORY   7

BOOK I

AUTHORITY   13

(Manifested and Recognized)

BOOK II

AUTHORITY   56

(Vindicated and Defined)

BOOK III

THE CHURCH   93

Foundations and Institutes

INDEX   153

OF THE SUBJECTS OF POEMS,
AND BIBLE REFERENCES

"Thou, then our strength, Father of life and death,
To whom our thanks, our vows, ourselves we owe,
From me, Thy tenant of this fading breath,
Accept these lines which from Thy goodness flow,
And Thou, that wert Thy legal Prophet's muse,
Do not Thy praise in weaker strains refuse!"

SIR HENRY WOTTON

INTRODUCTORY

The idea, which appears to be gradually developed in that portion of the Gospel history dealt with in the first volume of this work, is embodied in the memorable declaration of the men of Samaria—this is indeed the Saviour of the world—with which *The Holy Infancy* closes.

That "He is Lord of all," the dominion, supremacy, the universal authority of our Lord appears to be the salient idea in this second volume. A careful study of the section here paraphrased leaves the reader convinced that the authority of our Lord was that attribute by which the Jews were during this period of the Ministry (between the first and second Passover) most profoundly impressed: and it may not be unprofitable to bear this fact in mind at a time when our conception of Christianity is lowered through a tendency to disregard the *Authority* of our Head.

The writer ventures to repeat some of the remarks which prefaced *The Holy Infancy*, adding this further plea for a rendering of the Gospel History in verse—that possibly the *incomparableness* of our Lord's Personality and Teaching could not be better exhibited than by even a feeble paraphrase (in verse) of the records we possess in the Gospels. Any life and teaching less than divine would shrink into insignificance if every recorded incident and saying were subjected to such treatment.

We are at present in a phase of religious thought when a synthetic study or the life and teaching of Christ may well be of use. If we could only get a whole conception of Christ's life among men, and of the philosophic method of His teaching, His own word should be fulfilled, and the Son of Man, lifted up, would draw all men unto himself.

It seems to the writer that verse offers a comparatively new medium in which to present the great theme. It is more impersonal, more condensed, and is capable of more reverent handling than is prose; and what

Wordsworth calls "the authentic comment" may be essayed in verse with more becoming diffidence. Again, the supreme moment of a very large number of lives—that in which a person is brought face to face with Christ—comes before us with great vividness in the gospel narratives; and it is possible to treat what we call dramatic situations with more force, and, at the same time, more reticence, in verse than in prose.

Indeed, the gospel story offers the epic of the ages for the poet who shall arise in the future, strong in faith, and meek enough to hold his creative gift in reverent subjection.

We know how the Tate and Brady version of the Psalms wrought a great religious revival, not only in England, but throughout Western Europe; we know, too, how Marot's Psalms fired the hearts of the Netherlanders to their heroic resistance. If new presentations of the Psalms have effected great things, what may not the Church expect when a poet shall be inspire to writ the epic of Christ?

It may be said, we have the whole story in the Gospels, and cannot hope or desire to improve upon that which is written. But this is true, also, of the Psalms; no poet's version can equal the original; a version in a new form is a concession to human infirmity, but we know how arresting a new, though inferior, presentation is; no one can read the Gospels in another tongue, though in a poorer translation, without new convictions, new delight. For these reasons, the writer ventures to hope that a rendering in verse which aims at no more than being faithful and reverent may give pleasure to Christian people, may help to bring out the philosophical sequence of our Lord's teaching, and throw into relief the incidents of His life.

The writer, at any rate, experiences in the study a curious and delightful sense of harmonious development, of the rounding out of each incident, of the progressive unfolding which characterises our Lord's teaching; and perhaps some measure of this entrancing interest may have found its way into this little volume. If this attempt send any one back to a more diligent and delighted perusal of the sacred text, its end will be fully accomplished, for then it will prove an aid to meditation in the closet and to teaching in the class.

The scope of this work, *The Saviour of the World*, is to cover each incident and each saying in a single poem, blank verse or rhymed stanza, according to the subject. The poems follow one another in a time sequence, but each is distinct and separable. Therefore, though the work will, God willing, continue through a series of little Christmas volumes, each volume will be complete in itself and independent of the rest.

The writer begs to acknowledge her great indebtedness to the Rev. C. C. James's *Gospel History*, combining the four Gospels (in the words of the Revised Version), which she has followed for the chronological order of events.

CHARLOTTE MASON

THE SAVIOUR OF THE WORLD

Volume 1: The Holy Infancy

ANGELS and prophets had long searched in vain
Those mysteries, now, for wayfarers writ plain:

How Christ was born in Bethlehem of pure Maid;
How to three kings His Rising was displayed:

How holy Simeon blessed him and foretold
His Mother's grief, He, sacrificed and sold.

How out of Egypt did God call His Son
That all the prophets figured might be done.

How, simple Child, He dwelt in Galilee
That simple folk His light might daily see.

How to Jerusalem in His Twelfth year
He went, before Jehovah to appear:

How there He shed His light, a duteous Boy;
To keep the law his errand, not destroy.

How eighteen years of meek submission, then,
Prepared Him for His labours amongst men.

How He went out to John to be baptized
And John in Him a Greater recognised.

How in the wilderness for Forty Days
He bare assaults of Satan. Give we praise!

How in Cana He made the water wine
That men should see of life in Him a sign.
How in Jerusalem quick drave He forth
The traders and their wares—of how small worth!

How Nicodemus heard of that new birth
Wherefrom grown man as little child comes forth.

How journeying north to Galilee once more,
He sate and taught that Woman heavenly lore.

How all the men came out who heard His fame,
And, SAVIOUR OF THE WORLD, *did Him proclaim.*

These things have we considered as we might
And hence would meekly follow in His light.

BOOK I

AUTHORITY

(MANIFESTED AND RECOGNIZED)

"He is Lord of all."

I

CHRIST HEALS THE NOBLEMAN'S SON

ONE further stage trod in His heavy Way
(Stage marked by signpost bearing Name of Grace,
THE SAVIOUR OF THE WORLD), the Christ goes forth
In Galilee once more: Himself hath said
That not amongst His own hath prophet praise;
He came to the Jews, and they received Him not:
In Galilee a rumour went abroad
Of His advance, and all the people wait,
Had they not seen signs in Jerusalem?

Again He came to Cana, where was shown
That sign of water sudden turned to wine.
A nobleman was there, by office held,
A Jew attached to Herod Tetrarch's court,
A Sadducee, belike, as courtiers were:
Now, in Capernaum lay sick unto death,
This man's young son: "Lo, here, the prophet, come
"From Jerusalem, men's mouths proclaim of God.
"Might a man's son be snatched from jaws of death
"By such an one wielding the power of God—
"If God there be—and here, a case to test:
"If God there be, and if God pity men,
"He will not let my young son's life blow out
"As lamp in th' wind—ne'er to be lighted more."
He came to Christ, and, all his pride forgot,
Prostate, besought Him for this one dear life
As a man prays to God, nor ever knew
His prayer, offense; who wonders seek and signs—

"'Tis not for these to know the power of God.
"Nay, ye will not believe except ye see
"Sign for amazement." Ever as He goes,

THE SAVIOUR OF THE WORLD, in casual way,
Drops word of our Salvation, links of chain
Let down to draw us from nether hell
Which is but our own self to itself left;
"To believe is to be saved, but ye must will;"
"I will," we cry, and haste to make resolve,
Spin ropes of sand can bear no work-day strain,
Because we give not that is asked of us;
Act of attention, not act of resolve,
The high demand; think we upon the Lord,
His ways of sweetness and His words of power,
Lo, we escape hell-fire, consuming souls
Aflame with desire for things that good they hold,
Fleeing their Peace the while! Attention, Soul!

The man knows not he is rebuked of Christ;
If e'en he hear, he heeds not: "Sir," he cries,
That father in distress, "Pray, Sir, come down,
"Or while I plead my young son will have died!"

And His compassions fail not: "Go thy way"
(Thus friendly spake the Lord to the poor man)
"Go thy way, thy son liveth:" meek he goes,
Hushed all his pagan clamour for a sign,
The word of Christ enough, once seen, His face.
He went his way down to Capernaum;
And as he went, his servants came with news,
"The danger's o'er, thy young son is restored!"
"When came the change?" he asked; no longer now
His cherished child has sole place in his thought;
"At seventh hour yesterday the fever passed."
The father saw, at that same seventh hour,
Him suppliant, and Christ compassionate;
And faith in flood came surging o'er his soul:
Not signs nor wonders now, but only Christ,
His heart desired; and that day and the next

The Spirit stirred in the dry bones of his life;
New birth had come to him; Christ had he seen;
Old things, ambitions, rancours passed away;
And home he went, simple as a little child,
To embrace the son given back at word of Him
In whose hand is our life. His servants saw
a new man in their master; heard at large
How child of all their hopes had been restored;
And at the master's flame each lit his torch:—
Lo, here a house, the first that served the Lord!
The child,—cried he "Hosanna" with the rest?
The man believed—what was it he believed?
Nothing can act, they say, but where it is:
Then what had acted on the sick boy's frame,
Driven forth his malady, restored sweet life
At word of Him who spake? And who was He?
He might not put in words the thing he knew—
this Galilean noble; in dim sort,
"GOD IS A SPIRIT," was revealed to him,
"Who goeth where He listeth, none to see:
"And He that spake the word, was He True God?"

II

CHRIST PREACHES AT NAZARETH AND IS REJECTED

NEWS comes to Christ of John delivered up;
And yet the more He went about and preached,
Urged by the Spirit, throughout Galilee.
In all the villages men talked of Him
And in the towns, wherever two or three
Gathered in a little group;—What think ye then
Of prophet in our midst who thus and thus
Hath done and spoken only yesterday?
There was none other talk in all those parts.

So, as He went from place to place, He taught
Ever, as custom was, in synagogue,
An open teaching every man might hear;
Came He to Nazareth where He was brought up:
Entering the synagogue on Sabbath day,
As was His wont, He stood, the usual way
Of one prepared to read: attendant came
And brought Him roll of book assigned that day,
Book of the Prophet Isaiah; straight He took,
And found the place where it is written, thus:
"The Spirit of the Lord on me is come;
"He hath anointed me to preach good news
"To all the poor; to captives liberty;
"Recovered sight to them who have no light;
"That happy year when God shall walk with men
"To proclaim to whomso'er hath ear to hear."

The words, how many a Sabbath had they heard,
Were new this day, as never heard before!
All eyes were fastened on the Reader's face;
And people knew a word had come to them,
Not from the parchment roll, but from His lips

Of whom the prophet spake so gracious words.
And when He closed the book and gave it back
To him in attendance, and sat down to teach,
Hung they all on His words as very meat
Morsel by morsel dropped in famished mouths.
"This day," saith He, "this Scripture is fulfilled
"In all men's ears." What more, we know not: here,
The Secret, had they wit to know. Not eye
Fed on the pride of life, nor greedy mouth,
Nor grasping hands all covetous of good:—
The ear shall carry healing for our hurt;
The WORD shall bring good tidings to the poor;
Shall loose the bonds of captives chained to dreams;
Shall ope the eyes of him who sees amiss,—
Sees little things as great, that which is not
As filling space and standing in the way;—
Shall heal the bruised soul, fretting in chain
Of vicious habit corroding the hurt life.
They looked for glorious era of Messias?
Messias is the WORD should set them free!
And every man bare witness in himself,
As words of grace, such words as no man spake
Since the world was, fell, healing, on his ear
And proved them to his heart the very words
That all his days he had been waiting for
As child at show waits for the curtain's rise:
Hunger, agape, was filled with words of life;
What matter for the rest when here was all?

Alas for that uneasy sea each man
Carries in his own breast! Now is the cry,
"Is this not Joseph's son, the man we know?
"Who gave him right to move with mighty words
"And send poor souls away full as from feast?
"What be his words to us? Away with him!"
He takes up their own word—common proverb,

"Physician, heal thyself!" (how good it is,
Endearing, human, in our Lord to use
Those pithy texts in which the people wrap
Wisdom of ages,—glorified by Him),
"Ye say, not words we want, but do thou here
"In thine own country where thou wast brought up
"Such mighty works as in Capernaum."

Nay, but, another word of theirs shows cause—
(Both proverbs issuing from bitter hearts)—
And He said: "Verily, to you I say,
"Your own hard word is true; no prophet can
"Do that for his own, for others he may work;
"His own will not accept him; goes he forth
"To strangers for the liberal mind, frank trust,
"Alone makes possible his mighty works.
"Was it not so of old? In truth, I say,
"Full many widows were in Israel
"In days when Elijah closed the heavens up
"And famine fell on the land: but not to these,
"To her of Zarapeth, widow of Sidon,
"Was Prophet sent. And, in Elisha's day,
"Israel had many lepers; none was cleansed
"But Syrian Naaman!" The word went home;
They knew themselves condemned, a faithless crew
With hearts too shallow to hold word of God:
As trees by summer breeze swayed to and fro,
Hearts of the people but an instant past;
As trees uprooted, whirled with fury on
Whither they know not, devastating all,
The furious crowd uprose and thrust Him forth,
(Whose words but now had dropped as tender dew
On hearts burnt up and parched of the world);
Now forth from synagogue, from city forth,
Proud city, set on hill, to brow of hill
In headlong passion, brought, to hurl Him down

That precipice behind the town, whence none
Could be cast down and live. For what? The truth,—
Capernaum readier for the Word than they;
Strangers more graced than Jews, for they were fit,—
Intolerable truth to men who lived
Bolstered with national pride, impervious
To searching words discovering each man's sin.
How 'scaped the Lord? He, passing through the midst,
Went on His way. We very well know how:
Just so, through imminent peril, brings He us.
Christ teaches in Galilee

III

CHRIST TEACHES IN GALILEE

THE Son of Man rejected is of men;
Again to His own He comes and they refuse:
Nor calls He fire from Heaven on guilty heads,
But patient, seeks Capernaum by the sea,
Bordering on Zebulon and Naphtali,—
Obedient to instructions set for Him:
Had not Esaias marked this stage of the way?
"Land of Zebulon, land of Naphtali,
"Toward the sea beyond Jordan, Galilee,
"Where Gentiles in the darkness saw great light;
"To them that sat in regions desolate—
"Where shadow of death broods over every man—"
And, as in house where corse lies waiting still,
No effort in that chilling presence is,—
"To them did Light spring up." They saw, arose,
Went each about his several business
With easeful heart as man who knows his way.
And in and out amongst them went the Light,
Searching dark corners out and hidden ways,
Preaching,—Repent, God's Kingdom is at hand,
And men must turn them from their evil thoughts
Or, light of the kingdom fallen across the land
Will from their eyes remove, and they sit in the dark
As in those years before they saw the Light;
But worse, for light withdrawn leaves deeper gloom.

IV

CALL OF THE FOUR FISHERS

WHERE then were the disciples all these days,
The five who followed from Jerusalem?
Might they not enter Sychar for the Jews,
Or, had two kept with Him, the three, gone home?
Of heart, what searchings had they in the days
They waited for a sign, a word from Him!
The people glorified Him in their ears;
And they—as men of great one graced with speech
Half doubt they dreamt the honour put on them,
Are sure they may not trespass on his grace,—
Thus diffident the three hung back from Christ,
Their souls afire with great desire for Him,
their searching thoughts busy about His words:
Had they done right to leave him? Were they wrong?
Had He desired their constant company
Or should they weary Him by following?
Again, their fishing and those family claims,—
Peter's, wife and her mother; his father, John's—
Might these in truth be lightly put aside?
We all know doubt at parting of the ways;
We would go right, but whither is the right?
We wait a sign, and comes. So, Jesus came
To Simon Peter and his brother Andrew:
Passing along by Sea of Galilee,
He saw the brothers cast a net therein,
For they were fishers: and the Lord—to whom
The things of Nature and the ways of men
As parables and mimic pictures shew
Of that true world of the spirit where is God,—
Saith unto them, "Come ye and follow me;
"Ye shall be fishers still; henceforth shall ye
"Draw men, not fishes, in a mighty net."

Straightway they left the nets and followed Him,
Their doubts at rest, their way made plain thenceforth,
Their hearts elate at mandate of their Lord!

A little further saw he other two,
Brothers and fishers also like to these;
Zebadee and his two sons James and John
Sat peaceful in their boat, mending their nets.
He called the brothers; straightway they gat up,
Leaving their father with his hired servants,
And followed Him, the Master of their choice;—
Not John alone, but James, by zeal of him
Fired with love of the Lord. Had he not heard
Of all that Jesus began to do and teach
In Jerusalem and by Bethabara,
And how the Baptist named Him, "Lamb of God"?

V

AUTHORITY OF THE LORD: THE DEMONIAC DELIVERED

WITH authority had Jesus called the four,
Had bidden water that it wine became,
Had cleansed the temple, taught successive crowds
A power may be in the world a thousand years
And none discern it—know to give it name;
But he who finds that latent property,
And knows to name it, he doth serve the world!

And thou, Capernaum, lifted up to heaven,
To thee 'twas given to discern that note
Unheard 'mongst men till Jesus came and spake!
In synagogue 'twas heard that Sabbath day
When Jesus straightway entered in and taught,
And, lo, thy folk, astonished, could tell why!
AUTHORITY, they said, was in their midst,—
The absolute "I say," I, who know all!
Not thus their scribes them taught: "Moses hath said,"
"The Fathers," or, "the Prophets"; never, I.
Nor satrap, monarch, wise man of them all
Since time began had dared thus forth to stand,
Absolute, and teach men the thing he knew
Untaught of any, fixed as firmament!
Now this did Jesus only among men;
They of Capernaum had the grace to know
And give fit name to attribute in Him
Which no man shared or shall share. Grace to thee,
Thou city greatly honoured, and how fallen!
We, who come after, grieve, nor mayest forget
That thou discerned Christ's Authority,
And taught us how to name that thou didst see!

To him that hath is given; seeing much,
City high-graced, Capernaum saw ope
Another vista of dominion, ruled
By sole authority of the Son of Man!
A man beheld He in the synagogue
Which had a spirit of an unclean fiend:
(Be there now left no foul-mouthed, filthy souls
Would seem to have given them up to unclean works,
Who ope their lips to gibe, nor care at what?)
And here a chance to lay a snare for Christ
And vex the souls of the rulers. So he cries,
That soul unclean, "I know thee who thou art,
"Jesus of Nazareth; ah, what have we
"To do with thee, thou Holy One of God?
"Art come us to destroy before the time?"
Jesus, who knew, addressed Him to the fiend
In occupancy of that house of soul;—
Rebuking him, He said, "Hold thou thy peace;
Come out of him." And, lo, that ghost, unclean,
In their midst threw him down, convulsing him,
Cried out with a loud voice, and then—came out,
Leaving the man unhurt! "Why, 'twas no more
"Than epileptic fit; the man came to
"In natural course;" wise in our generation,
We explain: thus, any fool can tell by clock,—
"Now it is night," nor ever stop to think
The earth has turned his place from source of light:
So, "epilepsy" satisfies today,
A name as good as any other: but the cause,
Mysterious play of good and evil thoughts
On bodily conditions, what know we
Of this, or, how beleaguered soul succumbs
To powers of evil sitting at his gates?
But this we know: when rage and hate get in
To our poor shattered keep, then, as a flood,
the enemy o'erwhelms; we are possessed;

Our thoughts are not our own, scarce so, our words;
Quick may we be hurried to awful deed
If habitude of prayer be not with us:
But if we cry on Him endured as we,
Lo, sweet and sudden peace possesseth us!
The flood of evil hath ebbed forth: we lie
Calm and restored at the dear feet of God!
Let him who never knew the like of this
Scoff at "possession" as were a dream of fools!
They of Capernaum, 'ware of the devil,
Saw this sign with amazement; questioned
Among themselves,—"New teaching! What is this?
"With Authority and power commandeth He
"The unclean spirits; and they, too, obey
"His word and straight come out! What thing is this?"
Ah, happy dwellers in Capernaum
To whom was secret of our peace made known,—
That at the word of Christ all ill possession,
All lust and sloth, all malice, envy, greed,
Steal forth as vanquished leaguers,—leaving PEACE!

And straightway the report of Him went out
Through all the villages and towns about.

Who, seeing apple fall, discerned straightway
That law which keeps the worlds in ordered place,
And knew to give it name, deserves our praise:
Grace to thee, fallen city, more, hast done!
Thou didst discern that Potency undreamed
Of men, the secret of our peace, and knew
To give it title due, Authority—
That which no man had used in his own right
Till Jesus walked the plains of Galilee,
Hill country of Judaea, taught in towns:
Men were there who had acted in God's name
Wisely and well: were those who had usurped

The place and power Divine; killed and enslaved,
Enriched and magnified, e'en as they would:
Capernaum distinguished Him from these:
Thou has graced us with a gift, Capernaum!

PETER'S WIFE'S MOTHER HEALED

WEARIED with that outgoing of Himself,
Attends all strenuous healing, teaching, work,
Jesus arose, and followed Him the four,
The fishers whom He loved, to Simon's house,—
Honoured to shelter Him, the King of men,
Simon was married, shared his family life
With his wife's mother: desperately sick
In burning fever lay she; and straight, they,
Simon and Andrew, James and John, the four,
Tell of the suffering woman, and beseech,
Remembering those signs they'd seen, that He
Would raise up their sick friend; whom when He saw,
He came (how gracious!) and stood over her,—
Compassionate of fevered tossing frame,
Of burning lips, of horrid misery,—
And He rebuked the fever. Forth it went,
Dismayed before the Lord, the Giver of life;
He took her by the hand and she uprose,
Not lifted by the strong men standing round,
Not spent with fever, weak as shaking lamb,
But, all her power of life restored in her,
Raised by His hand, she gat up, grateful, glad,
And served the simple meal—her offering.

In darkness lie we, in the shadow of death;
Fast bound in misery and iron, see
Or mother, wife or child, husband or son
Grow sick, bear anguish, die, and leave us here!
And that sick woman, raised from off her bed,
Able to minister in that same hour,—
What comfort here for us? Nay, sorer grief,—
Our dearest thus tormented—this one saved!

Not thus the tale moves Christian heart, grown meek:
No longer battered by wild sea of life
'Gainst horrid senseless crags that break us quite,
But, thrust with violence upon the breast of God,
Why, if He will, we suffer, die, or live;
Not this, the end: meanwhile, we pray alway:
What myriads live gladly on to-day
For that their friends have prayed, and He hath heard!
Alway, He hears,—if, loving us, He purge
With pain or sanctify through sorrow;
"Yea, though He slay me, will I trust in Him!"

At Even Ere the Sun Was Set

THERE came that day from heaven a Shining One,
The Angel of the Presence men call Hope;
He bent o'er beds where men had languished long,
Where little children suffered, women moaned:
And, as these heard what Christ had done that day,—
Of Simon's mother and that demoniac,
And as friends promised to take each to Christ,
Why, what a Sabbath of the Suffering, that!
But not till even might these be carried forth
These many ailing: Sabbath must be kept;
And through the long tense hours they watch and wait:
Behold, the sun is setting! Forth they go
From many a door, the sick and they that bare,
Piteous procession, all elate with hope!
Round Simon's door each group laid down their sick
To wait till He came forth; and all the folk
Gathered there, too, to wait, made way for these
With words and looks of pity—such a sight!
Now HE came out, and saw, and suffered all;
Himself took our infirmities, 'twas said,
And by His stripes we're healed: Isaiah's words.
Diverse diseases gathered at the door,
And they possessed of evil spirits; all
Drained His divine compassion, drank His life;
On every one of them He laid His hands,
And all were healed by that Sacrament,
His touch upon them. Restless spirits, too,
Were cast out with a word, nor let to say
They knew Him, Son of God. With authority,
He drave out all the harms that hurt the flesh,
Ills worse that hurt the spirit; and men knew
"He maketh whole, the Healer of mankind!"

Quick reaped Capernaum reward of faith;
In the morn knew she Authority was His,
And lo, at eve, her sick folk all restore!
His wages tarry not, WHO hireth us!

VIII

JESUS PRAYS IN THE DESERT

THE Son of Man a great while before day
Went out in th' dark to seek where He might pray
He bare out sicknesses—the burden pressed;
Took our infirmities—and was distressed,—
His mortal frame unequal to sustain
A whole world's miseries, all people's pain!

Renewing sought He at His Father's hand;
Cried to that Ear alone could understand
The pity of it all—fair men to see
Distorted, loathsome, in their misery!
For never Christ resigned Himself to bear
Diseases of mankind with easy care.

Never taught He poor sufferer to say,
"Tis by God's will I languish here to-day:"
But to the Fount of Healing men He led,
Whence flows or health, or hope, or easy bed,
Made of the Father for His suffering child—
Soothed in his pain, by tenderness beguiled.

The Father and the Son alone could gauge
That misery they concerted to assuage;
And the spent Son upon the Father draws
For mortal strength to use in mortal's cause,—
"My Father, pity suffering men," He prays,
"Restore Thine image in these evil days!"

And as He cried aloud in desert place
The sudden dawn illuminated tear-wet Face:
The night's distress passed from Him as a cloud
Flees from the rising sun; adoring bowed

Christ Jesus—"I rejoice to do Thy will,
"My Father, all Thy mind through me fulfill!"

Glorious as bridegroom moves He on His way,
With strength endued for all the destined day;
In greatness of His might the Saviour goes
Rejoicing, forth, to combat human woes:
The night's distress is past, and in its stead,
See, beams of grace and hope enray His head!

IX

IN GALILEE

THE LORD had need of all the grace of God,
Patience, strength, hope and courage for His work—
Those tempers that renew our mortal frame—
For Simon sought Him, with the rest, and cried,
Eager with spirit of the world's success,
"All men are seeking thee!" How good to him
That men should seek His master! Lo, he thought,
The work is half accomplished, Christ made King!
The multitudes arrived in desert place,
Claim property in Him, would hold Him back;
Nay, was He not their own? Had they not seen
First among men, Authority in Act?
The disciples standing by with swelling hearts
Augured great things from the crowd's urgency;
But Christ, who ne'er refused one supplicant's prayer,
Yet never yielded to the popular voice:
He knew what was in man, the frothy stuff
That goes to swell a crowd, a clamour raise:
Turning to His disciples,—"Let us go
"To all the towns about, that they may hear
"Good tidings of the kingdom; I must preach
"To other cities, too; for this, I came."
And Jesus went about in Galilee,
Taught in their synagogues and healed their sick.
Full many sick they brought to Him, sore diseased,
Tormented, palsied, or of fiends possessed,
And all of them He healed—all grievous ills
And loathsome, that destroyed men's soul or flesh—
He took the infirmities, the sickness bare,
In that new strength got in the desert place
Where power of God He sought for mortal frame
Exhausted under burden of men's ills.

Where'er He went, great multitudes pursued,
From Galilee, Judaea, Decapolis,
From beyond Jordan and Jerusalem;
All men had heard report of Him and came
So they might taste the sweetness of His words,
Might see the signs He wrought, and know for sure,
"Lo, God hath sent Messias unto men!"

X

THE FISHER'S NET

WEARIED with labours up and down the land,
The Saviour walks again by that loved lake,
Gennesareth the fair, whose mirror holds
The loveliness of earth, the hues of heaven:
And as He stood, the eager multitude,
An-hungered, holily, for Word of God,
Pressed close upon Him, that no crumb be lost
Of that soul's manna dropping as he went:
And He, aware as ever of men's needs,
How each man fain would hear, and pressed Him so
That, urged into deep water, some might drown,—
He looked for simple way, and saw two boats
Shored high and dry—the fishers had gone out
To wash their nets, the very four we know,
Not yet in constant waiting on their Lord,
But biding His commands from day to day.—
He entered Peter's boat, bade him put out
A little from the land that all might see,
Hear each word uttered in that resonant air.
Then He sat down and taught the multitudes.
His teaching done,—and every soul enmeshed
In that fine web of thought He cast abroad,
Whence, whoso would escape by violence
Must tear him from the strong enveloping truth,—
He turned to teach His fisher's craft to them
With Him in the boat. "Put out," He said, "to sea,
"And cast your nets for fish." Simon replied,
(Sure he knew his fisher's craft if naught beside!)
"Master, through all the night we toiled, nor took
"Aught for our labor;" caught he here a glance
Reproving his presumption—did he know
In truth, so very much of fishers' lore?

Meek, he goes on, "but at Thy word, my Lord,
"I will let down the nets." They did, and lo,
Great multitude of fishes they enclose,
With straining muscles, holding a breaking net,
And beckon to their partners in the boat
That lay alongside; these hasten to give help
And both the boats are filled to sinking point,
From that same deep, experience reckoned void!
But not their fishing was their Lord's concern;
Sign of the Kingdom gave he, parable;
Had they the grace to read? Rich haul forgot,
That ardent Peter fell at Jesus' knees,
And prayed Him, "Go, depart from me, O Lord,
For I, a sinful man, and Who art Thou,
But Very God in our midst, of cleaner eyes
Than to behold our sin!" Amazed was he,
The fishers, too, and James and John, his friends,
At draught of fishes taken at HIS word!
Full ready, Simon, to receive that word
Wrapped up in parable of breaking net,
Scarce strong to hold that multitude of fish
Driven to its meshes by one word from Him
Who knows the depths of seas, the deeps of hearts,
And sees the barren regions teem with life!
"Fear not," He said to Simon, "henceforth thou
Shalt catch, not fish, but men. The net I give,
Of mesh so delicate that scarce to touch
Or sight 'tis evident, so closely wove
That never fish so small it shall escape,
So strong, leviathan in vain would break,—
That net of My Church, behold thou shalt cast forth,
And gather to Me multitudes of men!"
In awe, they brought the boats to land, nor stayed
To count the fishes, gain a goodly price—
No price in all the world for them but that

"Well done" of His, should glorify all work!—
They brought their boats to land, left all behind,
(What spoil for Zebadee and the hired fishers!)
And followed wheresoever He should lead.

XI

THE LEPER HEALED

NOW, who is this that stands beyond the crowd
And strikes a hollow bell and cries aloud
At ominous intervals, "Unclean! Unclean!"
The shuddering people shrink from sight obscene,
A man all over leprous, all disease,
Whose touch defiling e'en the vilest flees.
Removed from men, an outcast and forlorn,
From all he loved, from all who loved him, torn,
Small wonder wretched leper haunts the spot
Where men assemble, though his awful lot—
To cry aloud lest any near him draw,
And, touching, put himself without the law.

What news is this the distant outcast hears
Of how unhappy men, released from fears,
The maimed, the halt, the sick, have been made sound?
Is there no hope for him? His woe profound,
Hath it no place of pity in the heart
Of Him who walks the ways, His blessed part,
To carry comfort to each suffering soul;
Is it that even he might be made whole
By single touch of those so gracious hands,
Or, by one word of His who health commands
With secret hope to living soul untold,
He tracks the Christ, that on occasion, bold
When fewer men are by, he might draw near
And urge His pity, work upon His fear
Of awful contact; to cleanse, were better, sure
Than risk corrupting touch with the impure!

Thus worked perhaps the mind whose body's state
Unlovely thoughts too well might generate.

40

He gat him close to Christ, fell on his face,
And worshipping, besought Him of His grace
To make him clean; for, saith he, "If thou wilt
"Thou canst remove this plague from me, my guilt!"
Ah me! This leper, justly doth he show,
The measure of our faith in hour of woe;
We too wait on our Lord with cries and tears,
"Thou canst, we know, but wilt remove our fears?"
Nor ever see His will is on our part
His mercy, quick t' alleviate our smart.
He can, He will, but is it for us to meet,—
Deliverance we cry for? Pity, sweet,
Went out towards that leper all decayed,
And fallen away from likeness God had made!

He stretched His hand to touch the loathsome thing,
And said, "I will; be clean:" quick healing bring
His officers of health; the wretched frame
All sudden is made sound, with flesh the same
He had as little child. Ah, happy soul
Beginning life anew all clean and whole!
Sure, every word of His grown dear to thee,
Thy life to His obedience thus set free,
Thou goest hence to serve Him as may be;
And He lays hest on thee, "See thou say
"Nothing to any man, but go thy way,
"Shew thyself to the priest, and offer things
"Which, by command of Moses, leper brings
"To witness to his cleansing." Glad, he goes,
Each small obedience precious, we suppose?
But who can judge that leprosy of heart,
Sin, we name it, wherein we all have part!
If any way be open save His way
Wilful, we make our choice to disobey.
In "man's first disobedience," share we all;
That little thing we're bidden works our fall!

Even so this leper, bid to hold his peace
Nor publish among men that vast release
Christ wrought for him, is quick to find good cause
For disobedience: "The leper draws,
If all men's loathing, yet their pity, too;
He feeds on alms; but what now must I do
A healthy man without the means to live?
If I proclaim my cure, all men will give,
Seeing me clean and sound, to hear the tale
Of how a word could cleanse; nor will they fail
To glorify Him who such wonder wrought;
No cause hath He then to complain of aught!"
And so the man went forth and spread the news
Of what Christ did for him; and hate pursues
Our merciful sweet Lord, who could no more
Enter a city for the jealous dread
Of scribes and priests lest all the folk be led
To follow Him, forsaking the dull round
Of rite and precept where no help was found.
to desert places went the Lord to hide;
In wilderness chose He to abide;
But multitudes from every quarter came
And brought their sick, their blind, their halt, their lame, --
Some for the healing impulse of His word,
And some to crave such cures as they had heard
Were wrought elsewhere: He taught and healed them all,
Heard, whosoever on His grace did call.
Then to remoter waste, His steps He bent,
Vigil to keep with God, for He was spent.

XII

JESUS HEALS THE MAN WITH THE PALSY

BEGINNING of the end, he brought to Christ,
That leper contumacious: lulled to rest
By His withdrawal, hatred lay awhile;
And after days had passed, again He sought
Capernaum by blue Gennesareth;
Not open teaching in the common ways
Was for Him now, but in a house he spake:
And doctors of the law were sitting by
From all the land and from Jerusalem;
Eager as sleuth-hounds following trail of blood,
They dogged His steps, laid wait upon His words,
From this time forth: the power of God to heal
The virulence of hatred and disease
Was present with them, and they heeded not.

That He was in their midst, the rumour spread;
Loyal Capernaum pressed to hear and see
Him, whom the people loved, so was no room
Left, not so much as space about the door;
To them He spake the word, nor heeded He
That those were sitting by, savour of death
Drew from His words of life. A stir outside
Caused men to turn their heads: "Now who comes in?"
None entered; by-and-by, above in roof,
The sound of tools, and lo, an open gap
Lets in the light of heaven; what is this?
A man let down on mattress by four cords,
Above, the hands of friends that lowered him,
Four eager faces, seeing all went right,—
And at the very feet of Christ he dropped,
This man with palsy; powerless he to move
Of his own wish, but by the grace of friends,

Sure, love for him made zealous in his cause;
Or else, content to turn from crowded door,
They'd borne their burden back, nor ever thought
Of breaking up the roof and through the tiles
Lowering the sick man to the very spot
Where Christ must needs behold him. Ever, He
Graces the plea of love; who cherisheth
Another's weal is sure to win His ear;
Jesus, beholding, saw their faith, their love
For their poor fellow held in living death!
Tender He spake to the sick of palsy: "Son,
Be of good cheer"—thou art released, stand up?
Nay, for He knew the man had worse within—
The gnawing, silent, never-ceasing hurt
Of those sins he had don: pathetic eyes
Spake less of deprivation than remorse:
And Jesus, knowing all, yet called him "Son,"
Raised of His mercy that abased soul,
And spake the word rests not with men to speak --
"Thy sins are forgiven thee." Authority
Spake once again as never in men's ears!
The hearers, what thought they? The palsied man
Knew in himself how that his plague was healed,
In joy of His forgiveness knew no lack,
Not lack of power in these poor moveless limbs—
Not lack of anything—his God atoned!
Had secret sin his malady ensured,
God knowing, and he knowing, none beside,
No, not the four who loved him and had faith?

Something they knew, those doctors of the law;
Sincerely shocked, they heard the awful words
Which let a soul loose from all his sins;
Cried "Blasphemy!" nor had they said amiss
Had He who spake those words been less than God.
"For who," said they, and therein they said well,

"Who but God only can forgive men's sins?"
And Jesus knew their thoughts (as knows He ours),
Perceived that righteous indignation cloaked
Inveterate malice pursuing still His life;
"Why think ye evil in your hearts," He saith,
Not for God's honour, but my ruin, lay
"Ye your heads together. Tell me this,
"Whether is easier, to this poor man
"To say, Thy sins be forgiven, or, Rise up and walk?"
"Easy enough," think they, with sneering lip,
"To say, Thy sins forgiven, for what's to show?
"Why any man might deal out hearts-ease thus,
"And none the wiser! But to claim this power
"Is blasphemy 'gainst God, and worthy death."
"Nay then," He saith, "and ye shall have a sign
"E'en for thy condemnation; ye shall know,
"The Son of Man on earth can sins forgive!"
Then, turning to the sick of palsy, saith:
"I say to thee, arise, take up thy bed
"And walk, thus laden, to thy house." He rose,
Before them all, took up his bed, went forth
To his house before them, glorifying God,
And the sweet grace of Him had sent him free
From twofold bondage on that blessed day!
No more we know of him, but sure a man,
So apt in his response to Christ's least word,
Forgat Him not, but followed Him and served,
Kept alway in the presence of that Power,
Knew to forgive his sin! All were amazed—
(The doctors of the law, people and priests,
Amazement held them fast), and praising God
Who had given such power to men, and filled with fear,—
"We've seen strange things to-day! Never till now
Hath man forgiven sin," they said, "and in sign
Of pardon, raised a palsied man to power!
This a new thing,—we never saw it thus!"

The sign we see not more; signs had their season,
Are there for us as for the men who saw;
Repeats He not the lesson He hath taught;
Ever as sign of the Kingdom, given by Christ
For men to con, remains it for all time;—
And paralytics are no more restored
As evidence that Christ forgiveth sin.

Above all grace, to Christ, dear was the Law,
Stern schoolmaster to whip poor souls to God!
While King may of his grace reprieve the wretch
Doomed for the coming morn, his clemency
Asserts, not abrogates, the general law:
Who sinneth he shall suffer—it is writ,
Else would men violate all sanctities!
The Law remains, no jot doth He forego;
But that best part, forgiveness, is for us,—
The Testament above the signature
Of witnesses who be of small account.

XIII

The Call of Levi

AGAIN Christ walked by the seaside;
The people flocked from far and wide
To hear the blessed words He spake
As slow He paced beside the lake.
And as He passed, He saw a man,
A much despised publican,
Who, heedless of his Jews estate,
In seat of Roman Customs sate
To gather from his nation pence
For Roman coffers—stern offence
To every patriotic Jew,
Who grudged to think the Roman drew
Or dues or honours from that land
Ruled only by Jehovah's hand!
Scorned of their race, such men took toll
Of moneys under their control,
Exacted than their due far more,
Grew rich upon ill-gotten store;
Grew rich, but failed to gain respect
And, prosperous, they met neglect.
But never yet was class so base
That in its ranks no single face
Witnessed a nobler, purer aim:
Close by this custom-house there came
The steps of Jesus many a day,
With following to hear Him say
Words of our life He ever dropped
Where'er He went, when'er He stopped:
Once and again had Levi heard,
From where he sat, the living word.
It fell upon an open mind,
And spread within that he might find

No place within, without, but there
This mighty word of God must bear
Sole rule o'er conduct, word, and thought,
O'er how he sold and how he bought,
No secret from this word was hid!
And Jesus, Who this great word spake
While treading margin of the lake,
Was He not Master of man's soul,
Entitled to supreme control?
But, publican, what hope had he
That this most sweet supremacy
Should over his poor sordid days
Take rule? He must pursue the ways
He'd learnt to tread: no shout of King
In heart of publican might ring:
Had he not sold himself for wage?
Nought left for him that thirst t'assuage—
That great God-hunger of the heart
In which the feeblest soul has part!
Poor Levi! know'st the Lord at last,
And art kept back by thine own past?

And lo, that day Christ spake one word,
Compelling happy soul who heard!
"Follow Me," said Christ, and Levi knew
Himself all known of Him,—the true
The false, the sordid, generous self
That longed for God and lived for pelf!
Christ knew it all, and, ah, sweet grace!
He called him from that hated place
Of customs, where he lost his soul
In gathering each paltry toll!
Quick rose he up with naught to say;
What to him now the coins that lay
In piles on table at his hand?
He followed his Lord's command,

Forsaking every lesser thing
In joy of summons from the King!

But not without a pang he went;—
Those others whom his lot had sent
For daily commerce to his seat,
Where publicans and sinners meet
To pay as others do their due,
Or else, exact from haughty Jew;
Could he be glad when these were left,
Of Israel's great hope bereft!
Levi bethought him what to do
That these poor friends might hear Him too.
A great feast made he, and sent out
His invitations round about,—
Not to men sought for and esteemed,
But to poor souls unworthy deemed
To touch the robes of righteous men;
Sinners and publicans were, then,
The guests he dared invite to meet
Messias! at his board to greet
The crowd of the disciples, too,—
Hungry for teaching, ever new.
How well he knew his Master's mind,
This new disciple! These, the kind
Of guests that most should please the Lord,
For these, most famished for His word!

Around the tables all took place,
And listened, wondering at the grace
Of every word the honoured Guest
Let fall among them, strangely blessed!
How many heavy burdens fell
From aching shoulders, who may tell,
As each, that word of life received!

But on the divans round the wall
Were guests, that waited not the call
Of invitation from the host;
At Eastern feast it is the boast
That whoso will may come and see:
And each man there, an enemy
Dogging His steps; each finger, mark,
Pointing in spite, each whisper, dark,
His condemnation bears to ear
Of neighbor, all too keen to hear!
"A Prophet, say you! Who are these
"With whom He eats and drinks, at ease?
"The men, publicans,—and women, faugh,
"The streets can tell you what they are!"
Remote the whisperers, but He heard,
And spake one soul-condemning word—
"The sick have need of healing, see,
"The good physician hastes; but ye
"Ye who are whole" (we hear His wrath
In mocking irony break forth),—
"Ye whole ones, ye that have no need,
"What do ye here 'midst this poor seed
"Of sick and sinful, patients all
"Whose needs on the physician call?"
But ye are here—go ye and learn
That word of prophet to discern!
Not sacrifice, your lavish gift,
But pity, that the weak shall lift,
Mercy to pardon, these to Me,
Saith God, the pleasing offerings be!
Lo, I came, not the good to call,
The satisfied, who cannot fall
From out their own complacency:
But sinners will I draw to Me;
Poor sinners, fain their God would find
That all their sin be left behind!"

XIV

THE JEWS ARE REJECTED

ANOTHER question rises, "See," say they,
"How John's disciples keep the Nation's fasts;
"Disciples of the Pharisees fast too,
"But thine, they eat and drink every day!"
How should He make them see a meaning here?
"The bridegroom in a house, do guests then fast?
"How can they so when he is with them there?
"Men fast for sorrow, not for bridal joy:
"A Bridegroom come I, my disciples, these,
"Foreshadow they the Bride; how can they fast
"While with them is the Bridegroom? Days will come
"When the Bridegroom is taken from them, fast will they!"
But what to the Jews the Bridegroom and His Bride
Joy of the infant Church, Christ in her midst,
And bitter sorrow on that bitter day
Should see Him crucified on Calvary!
Nor disciples nor the Jews could understand,
But present to the Master's thought alway
That awful consummation! Good for them
Then to remember, Christ knew how they would fast
And weep, all orphan'd and alone, for Him

As traveller brought to stand at fall of night
By monstrous face of cliff right in his path,
Unbroken, sheer, of height impassable,—
With never lodgment for adventurous foot,
No unsuspected defile breaking through,
And, stretching far and wide, on either hand,
No hope to round it;—so precipitous
And blank as this rose before Christ a wall
At nightfall of His soul, wearied and faint
With sinners' contradiction! How surmount

Stupendous obstacle of Jewish pride,
Obstinate, prejudice, malice, greed, hate?
Nay, God Himself will not forever strive
Against determined enmity of man:
That day went judgment forth: (O take we heed!)
Not fit the nation of the Jews for grace
Of His Salvation; verdict from themselves,
(For men be their own judges), He pronounced,
In homely figures, might in memory lodge:—

The rottenness of that old Jewish Church
He pictured in plain parable for them;
That, which reform but tears to shreds, must waste
Till it shall fall to dust of sheer decay:—

> "No man doth take a garment old,
> Whose gaping rents invite the cold,
> And lay on each a patch of new
> And undressed cloth; whoso should do
> This foolish thing would make worse rent;
> The new would tear from that was spent,
> And ever, for his well-meant pains,
> The ragged garb worse hurt sustains,
> Till none may wear a thing so poor,
> Cast forth as refuse from the door."

Behold we here a key to all
To church or nation may befall;
Too weak to bear a just repair,
Loss and oblivion its share
In word as pregnant and as plain, proclaims
The Lord a further disability
Of the Jews for His salvation: narrow, they,
Constrained in limits inelastic, close,
Of the old thought had lost its vital force—
The power to spread and grow, expand, be free;

What place for living truth in hard dry shell
Which with new thought's expansion might not swell?

> "No man will put new wine in skin
> So hard and dry, ferment within
> Must crack the bottle will not yield,
> And spill the precious wine afield.
> The wise man taketh bottle new,
> Pours in contents with judgment true,
> Allowing space for all that stir
> And working agitates liquor
> Still instinct with the life it brought
> Seeking the sun as once it sought."

Lord, how shall our poor hearts and dry
Our narrow vessels, hold that high
Expanding, rising, living truth
Thou offerest us? In thy dear ruth
Grant us new hearts that shall contain
Wine of thy truth, for we are fain!
On one more charge the Lord condemns the Jews;
Those slaves to use and wont, change in itself
Was hateful to them, howe'er good the change:
Habited with a religion made to fit
Their eating, drinking, walking, prayer and praise,
All sacrifices, offerings, daily round,
Their Sabbath rites, behaviour at high feasts
In Temple held,—what then to do,
What was there not prescribed for in the Law?
Uneasy stirrings of a tottering wall
Moved them at words of His who little store
On the whole fabric of their life and thought
Would seem to set; whose words stirred other chords
Might set the whole vibrating, quick bring down
Their house about their heads; away with Him!

"Men that have drunk old wine despise the new;
They choose the creed they're used to, false or true!"

Thus on three several counts did Christ reject
The rulers of the Jews: their Church itself
Grown rotten past repair; individual minds,
Too narrow warped and dry to take the truth;
The habit of old custom in them,
Too strong to let them savour the new truth:
"Let be," saith He, who nations rules and men,
"No stewards of the wine of life are ye;
Not yours is the whole garment of My praise,
Nor yours to taste the cup of life I spill;
I leave you in the hardness of your heart:—
For other men, another Church, the part
Ye found not grace to fill: I make all new!"

How shall we stand when Thine own people fell?
Where they transgressed, what hope that we do well?
Saviour of sinners, grant us grace that we
'Scape these Thy condemnations, kept by Thee!

BOOK II

AUTHORITY

(VINDICATED AND DEFINED)

XV

THE MAN HEALED AT BETHESDA

SILENT and sad, the Master, occupied
With tactics of the warfare He must wage;
For, challenge given and taken, follow plans:
Captain of our Salvation, went He forth
With following to the Temple, to keep Feast.

Now, by the Sheep Gate is Bethesda's Pool;
Round it a loggia, graced with porticos;
And in these lay a multitude of sick,
Blind, halt and withered, contrast pitiful
To the structure's airy grace: Jerusalem
Poured out her misery on this fair spot;
And why? A gracious legend haunts the place—
Angel of God, descending, stirs the pool;
In jets the waters rise at periods due,
And lo, the water troubled, who first comes,
His malady is healed—he steps out whole!
Small wonder suffering folks should crowd the spot,
And friends should gather to help sufferers in;
And while they wait and watch for the red-spring's leap,
All gossip of the city goes the round.
A superstition, say we, idle dream?
We, too, know springs of healing, travel far
To dip in this or that one; wise are we;
Our fancy tarries not with angel-dream;—
Sulphur or iron, salts of various kinds,
These work our cure—what need have we of God
Or, those, His unseen ministrants, who serve
Where'er He worketh health or any grace?

And Jesus walked among them—saw, belike,
(For things that meet the eye, to Him, the shew

As in a figure of the real things);
The sick—those souls aweary of the world;
The blind—whose eyes were closed to Him, but saw
Matter and modes of outer universe;
The halt—whose progress is distressing-slow
In path that leads to God; the withered—
Dead souls and dry who knew no aspiration,
No gracious grief for sin. A certain man
For eight and thirty years was lying there;
And Christ, who deals with us men one by one,
Singled out him; eager, we wait result.
We know when Christ, our touchstone, finds a man
Straight he himself discovers, all he is:
Poor man, for half a life-time lying there!
Unwittingly we wish him all good speed—
That he may pass the certain tests applied
By every word of the Lord. Now Jesus knew
How long he'd been in that case, and saith to him—
That single question reaches every soul
With whom the Lord hath dealings—"*Wouldst* thou
In very deed be whole?" Men say, to-day,
"I would, alas! I were a better man!"—
A worthier father, mother, daughter, son,
But idle wishes may not climb the skies
Nor reach the ear of Him, the nations heals;
The active *will*—condition He exacts;
The will that strenuous bends a man's full force
To vigorous attention: there be sick
Today who will not bend an idle mind
To *think* on what should heal them,—work, or food,
Or free consumption of God's blessed air.
But how behaves this man—he surely wills,
Why else was there? He whines and takes Christ's words
In merited reproach; "Sir, I have none
To put me in the pool, the water, moved;
While I am coming, lo, some other man

Before me steppeth down." "Arise," saith Christ,
"Lift up thy bed and walk." Peevish complaint
Forgotten for the nonce, constrained by Christ,
The man, made whole, took up his bed and walked;
Nor ever turned to see who was't that healed,
Nor lifted praise to God. We know Him now.
'Twas Sabbath on that day: the vigilant Jews
Surrounded the man was cured: say they to him,
"To-day, the Sabbath, to take up thy bed,
This is against the law." Straight he replies,
"He bade me who made me whole." "And who is he?"
He that was healed wist not who made him whole;
A multitude was there, and, quiet act
Of healing done, Jesus had disappeared,
Lost in the crowd of many like-robed Jews.

"One like a Son of Man" had come that day;
From out his mouth proceeded a sharp sword,
Mere ritual and worship, cut in twain!
Controversy proceeded to Calvary
Grew definite that morn; removed had He
The keystone from that arch which held in place
Fabric of Jewish polity and rites:
Who bore a burden on the Sabbath day,
Stoning to death his due, ordained the Law:
Out of His way had gone the Son of Man
To cast this challenge down; the next day sure,
The next, and the day after he'd be there,
This impotent man: why heal on Sabbath day?
His time was come:—and henceforth goes He forth,
Dogged and pursued and wearied unto death
By virulent incessant enmity!
The man that was healed—was it in brave defence
He spoke of Him who bade him bear his bed?
The sequel shows. In the crisis of Christ's life
When He brake with Jewish sanctions, even then,

Leisure had He to think upon the man,
Ungrateful, He had healed; went after him,—
(With such persistence finds He thee or me),
And in the Temple found: to gift of health
His tested soul made no response of thanks;
How will he bide rebuke? Lo, here a sword
Divides our joints and marrow! All sweet souls
Are gentle under judgment, take reproof
As that which is their due; who will not bear
To know offence in them—unworthy found
By Him who holds the scales. "Thou art made whole,
"Go thou, and sin no more, lest some worse thing
"Come unto thee!" Instant the worse thing came:
Resentment like a flood o'erwhelmed his soul;
Ingrate before, vindictive turned he now:
To enemies of Christ he went in haste
And told them Who had healed him; played his part
In that dire tragedy for men was wrought!

XVI

1. THE ONENESS OF THE FATHER AND THE SON

THE issue narrowed to a single point,
Th' observance of the Sabbath, rage of the Jews
Gathered to head likewise; their enmity
Left Him no place of safety. What did He?
As with large frankness speaks a generous soul
Disclosing all his mind, his purpose whole,
Or, speaking for he must the thing he knows,
Compel'd by strong-swelling truth in his breast,
So Christ discloses to these men of hate
(Was it in Court of the Temple He thus spake?)
Ultimate mysteries of love and life!
As sudden break in heavy cloud reveals
Glories of gold and purple, so displayed
(Scarce conscious seeming of the things He shewed),
Messias, glories of the City of God!
Purple of amethyst, the sapphire's blue,
Jacinth and chrysoprase and emerald,
Lustre of stones most precious, modified
By luminous softening of the pearly gates,—
Such glories Christ revealed in meek defence,
Declaring why He wrought on Sabbath day:—

"My Father worketh hitherto, and I
"Work ever with the Father from the first:

"Ye claim the Sabbath sacred? So be it;
"But work is sacred also, is of God.

"How then shall holy thing mar holy thing
"And sacred work defile your sacred day?

61

"The works that I do ye may also do
"On Sabbath days and all days, they are good."

The blessedness of work, discovery,
Our very own, so think we, our chief prize;—
Nor wage, reward or praise, but only work,
The Gospel of our day of strenuous life;—
How good to know this joy we think we have won
Was shared by God and the Son ere worlds were made!
Defending work, yet deeper He offends;
For this cause sought the Jews the more to kill,—
"He brake the Sabbath, yea, and worse, He calls,
"The very GOD his Father, equal both!"

To those blind eyes, deaf ears, those halting steps,
Jesus unfolds that mystery of Oneness,
The Atonement with the Father that was His,
Atonement in whose ever-widening reach
All men should find the Father and be one!
Void of reserve, He shows the ties that bind—
Ties of diversity and unity—
The Divine Father and the Son Divine!
O wondrous condescension! Make us meet
To look and learn with open eyes and meek!

Subjection and obedience of the Son,
Pattern of all fit human ordering,—
"Nothing the Son can do, but that He seeth
"The Father also do; what things soe'er
"The Father doeth, likewise doth the Son."
Oneness of mind so perfect, could the Son
Or think a separate thought, do separate act?
All sin is separation; happiness,
Lies it not in perfection of accord?
In our small lives we know it; cross are we

With some poor neighbor of the least account
To us? How sore are we, remorseful, sad;
Why doth so small a matter vex our soul?
Not small th' offence although th' occasion small;
The Pattern of the Unity Divine
Constrained us not to follow; we were vexed;
Nor found our peace again till, sorry, we,
Seeing ourselves were wrong; then, little act
Of atonement makes us one with every man,
At one with Christ in God. Lord, help us keep
Thy Spirit's unity in bond of peace!

"The Father loves the Son and showeth Him
"All things that Himself doth." As when a king
Confides his mind to modest courtier
All gratified to learn the things that please,
Things that displease his lord, e'en so do we
Find confidence of Christ to gratify:
"Tis sweet to ponder how, as human son,
Promoted by his father's trust in him,
Is glad, so Christ in the Father's Love rejoiced,
Who showeth Him all He doth. Admitted, we,
To secret of those high relations
Subsisting 'twixt the Father and the Son,
Sure, we, too, learn of love and reverence.

All things the Father doeth, showeth He;—
Doth all the time for creatures of His hand;
The lily of the field restored by dew,
The sufferer recovered of his pain,
And such a thing as Christ but now had done,
Restored the impotent. What "greater works"
Lie in the thought of Christ? Belike, the three
Whom shortly He will wake from death, "that ye
"May marvel." This, of every sign the end,
To turn men's thoughts to Christ—Attend; my soul!

The Father raiseth from the dead all day
And every day, nor pauseth; life of plant,
Of insect, human life called from the void,—
What be all these but raisings from the dead?
And what, that mystic secret quickening
That stirs a soul to rise and go to God,
But a raising of the dead? Ultimate power
Of God the Father this, and this the Son
In equal measure shares; He quickeneth, too,
E'en who He will; no choice arbitrary,
For man, not pawn on chessboard moved about
E'en as the player wills; but *his* to will,—
Most high prerogative of human state,
And, willing with the Son who wills to quicken,
Behold, the man alive, *at one* with God!

XVII

CHRIST'S DEFENCE

2. OF JUDGMENT COMMITTED TO THE SON

SUBJECT unto the Father is the Son,
Nor will, nor act, can He apart from God.
Subject the Son for that the Father showeth,
And he that learns is subject to who teach:
One with the Father, for, as one They work,
Father and Son divine; equal, the Son
For work He doth, and for the life He holds;
The Father and the Son both raise the dead
And quicken who They will.
                              Diversity
Of operation next proclaims the Son;
A separate power, ceded of God to Him,
The power of judging men, reveals He now;
"Neither the Father judgeth any man,
"All judgment hath He laid upon the Son."—
Touched with the sense of our infirmities,
That Judge whom all men know behind the door
Reproving or commending every hour;
Reproving, not to punish, will we hear!

Not waiting for a fatal day of doom
Us and our sins to away with, but at hand,
That quick and powerful Word, discerning thoughts,
Intents of heart and every hidden thing!—
O wonderful, Saviour and Judge in One!
As though the Judge austere stepped down from Bench,
Laid hand on prisoner's shoulder in the dock,
"Guilty art thou; but trust in me for all,
"Myself will bear all if thou canst but trust!"
Poor wretch, he looks on clement countenance,

And trusts, how can he other, all to him,—
And loving him who saved, a new man, he!

And why this royal crown of judgment placed
On the head of the Almighty Son? He tells:
"Equal in work, in power, in unity,
"Equal in honour must be Son and Father;
"Who knoweth not the Son, how honours he
"The Father, sent Him forth, Ambassador?"
Now writhed the Jews in agony of hate!
"Blasphemy, nay, and double blasphemy!"
The exceeding boldness of this claim of Christ
To equal state with the Father, how impugn?
No words more strong assurance might convey:
For all who love Him, sure, the final word
Spake Christ that day. Alas, for wilfulness
Of wayward human heart! That stumbling-block
Which vexed the Jews vexes the Church today;
Has vexed throughout the ages! "Honour we,"
Say men to-day, "the Father, who is God.
"And Christ, we hold a very blameless man,
"Set for our imitation and our praise."
While other some, to "Jesus only" owe
Salvation gotten grudgingly, with pains,
From the Father's slow consent! And love grows cold
In them that choose the Father, not the Son:
Alone to worship. For our sake, the Lord
Claims equal honour, not more, no! not less;
Ambassador from Heaven, hear Him announce—
"Who honoureth not the Son, hear Him announce—
"Who honoureth not the Son, he honoureth not
"The Father which hath sent Him." This, the law.

"Nay, fear not, humble souls that hear My Word
"And tremble at the Judgment. Verily,
"Who hears My Word and, in that Spoken Word,

"Hears and believes the Father Me hath sent,
"No judgment is for him; and what is death?
"A corner turned in that long way of life
"Already he is treading every day:
"Eternal life is for this man begun;
"His passage out of death hath he performed;
"Believing in the Father and the Son,
"Honouring with equal honour, Father, Son,
"What judgment now for him, at one with God!"
Ah, happy folk who hung about and heard
The voice of Jesus as He spake the Word!
For us, a lesser joy; we speak, He hears,
Vouchsafes most tender answer to our prayer;
But, oh, to hear Him speak! Not in the page
Holding the written Word, but living Voice
Speaking to living ear! Nay, is not this
Commerce of speech betwixt ourselves and Him,
Of those good things He giveth without stint?
We speak, He hears, and *speaks to us again*!

XVIII

CHRIST'S DEFENCE

3. OF LIFE

YET more hath He to speak: "Hard doctrine," say ye,
"Give us the simple Gospel tale we know!"
Is it indeed so simple? Not too hard
For simple sincere soul who earnest hears;
But hard, too hard, for lighter thought of the learned,—
This single lore concerns a man to know;
A lore, takes a man's life to comprehend
E'en its first elements!
              He spake of Life,—
Unhindered, exquisite, that mounts and sings,
Glad as a child and careless as a bird!
But, life to them who heard? A weary moil,
Incessant struggle for some bauble joy
When not contention for the bread they ate!
"In Him was life,"—nay, what was that to them?
Life of their hand was all their thought embraced,
And that they had for getting. Quick to see
They knew not what He said, Christ turns to that
Familiar theme which points the lives of men,—
Death, the dread period of our days. "In truth,

"The life I tell you of is that same life
"Ye know in daily living; death, that death,
"That perishing in darkness of the grave,
"Whereof the awful fear haunts souls of men.
"That ye may see what meaneth death and life,
"Behold, the hour is near when senseless souls,
"Those ye name dead, even those shall hear the Voice
"Of the Son of God, and they that hear shall live!
"Ye marvel at this, but, lo, that hour draws nigh

"When all the dead, the dead of ages past,
"Shall hear that Voice, obey that potent cry,
"From the Son of Man shall issue."

                                     All come forth,
The good and ill alike; those have done ill
To face the ill they did—the judgment, hear!
The Dead who well have done—to return at will,
Unseen, unheard, unfelt, all unperceived?
(What sense has flesh a spirit to discern,—
Shall clumsy rites and tricks in darkness serve?)
Enter they as they will all joys of Earth—
All knowledge and all beauty, cast abroad,
Too small, too high, remote, for man's poor eyes?
And all the help they meant and could not bring,
This, their reward? Their service to the King?

XIV

THE WORLD TO COME (THE DISCIPLE)

A CHILD will play all day at what he'll do,—
        "When I am big!
        "Great hunter will I be!
        "That field I'll dig!"
His parents look on smiling while he plays,
And with bewildering changes shapes his days.

And we, poor foolish, when we dream and say
        "Thus shall it be,—
        "Our Father worketh yet,
        "And shall not we?
"Not eager, we, for crowns nor crystal seas,
"Or harps or singing or eternal ease;

"We would be doing as our Father doth!—
        "We have no fears;
        "With all our puny might
        "Would roll His spheres!"
Sure, not for this severely will He chide,
Our Father, who for love of us hath died!

"Ye shall go before your brethren and help
them, until the Lord hath given your brethren rest."

"O the dear world, sweet life, congenial joys!
        How give them up?
        Though all be sin-defiled,
        Where find we else
The promise we believe our longings hold,—
What work for us in any other fold?

All bright may glow the joys of other spheres,
But this, our home!
And would we barter it
For any gain,
Poorer, less constant, had our substance grown:
Jesus, in separate joy, were less our own.

Continuance, sure, belongs to higher life;
All fickleness,
All change, with Death must pass,
And leave us true:
Less a new life than utmost scope in this,
With help laid on us here, ah, hope of bliss!

Jealous are we, with jealousy unreasoning,
Over their joys;
For their gain, sadly bear
Unbidden loss:
With Him;—in Him;—there all the promise ends:
Ourselves, not Christ, do banish our sweet friends.

Sure, the dim kingdom where we seat our Dead
Is of the world:
The heaven of Christ is ruled
By other laws:
Not cumbrous change in circumstance and place,
But the enraptured vision of His face!

Death opes not heaven's gate; for long ago,
Soon as the King
Shone in upon the soul
Did heaven begin:
A blessed state, a lifting up forever;
Not some far seats when soul and body sever:

Two fuller consummations be there yet
                    To this full bliss:—
                    Our holy dead have reached
                    The second life,—
When pure eyes see the King in beauty fresh,
And service bears no dragging clog of flesh.

Then to live out all possibilities
                    Of love and help,
                    Of counsel and support,
                    That now but mock
These slow unloving wills: to be unseen
Among our own beloved, a ghostly screen,

And love them with love purely purged from self,
                    That, as an air
                    Tender, should wrap their lives,
                    Nor ever fret
With any waywardness: to lay their cares,
And with pure spirit-promptings, help their prayers,—

What life were this! Nor only for our own
                    Would we have help
                    Laid on us, but for all
                    Whose pain now moves,
Whose thoughts inspire,—all life that any way,
If only in fond dream, on ours doth play.

And not unowned, or self-imposed, our tasks;
                    Ever bidden
                    By the dear Word of God
                    Willing His will,
In the low rest of meekness, were our ease:
So, working, should we yet from labours cease.

* * * * *

Poor, ignorant and foolish, what know we
　　　　　If this may be,
　　　　　Or, other, better life?
　　　　　We trust in Thee!
Our Father, wilt not smile on us and say,
"Tis but my silly children at their play?"

XX

CHRIST'S DEFENCE

4. THE WITNESSES. CONDEMNATION OF THE JEWS

IN pigmy arrogance we strut and cry
Of independence: yielding, we, to none!
"I can do nothing of Myself," saith Christ,
"No, not that judging I but now affirmed,
"For, as I hear, I judge." What hear'st Thou, Lord?
Battle of argument, vain, noisy, vexed?
Nay, there be Three who work, Eternal One:
"The Spirit of the Lord doth rest on Me,
Spirit of understanding, knowledge, might,
And of good counsel. He wakeneth day by day,
Morning by morn, Mine ear to hear the truth;
And, as I hear, I judge: My judgment, right,—
For not My will I seek." Here, a new thing;
Gods of the heathen, wilful are they all,
E'en as they please, they do, because they choose:
Jehovah's Self, as the Jews interpret Him,
Arbitrary as are the Nations' gods:
All men are as the gods conceived of them;
Arrogant, wilful men have such a god
As suits their mood; only in Christ, we say,
"I seek not mine own will, guide Thou my way!"
Here, test for our decisions, great and small;—
Seek we our will? Not righteously we judge!
Seek we the will of God, hearken we, too,
To Spirit of Counsel at our ear?
So may we trust our purpose and go on.

Behold our Lord's defence,—that thesis nailed
Before the eyes of all men then and now:
Those arguments that show Him one with God;

Claiming Authority as natural right;
Able God's innermost counsel to reveal!—
We could have done it better, so we think,
Loftier the proofs of His divinity
That we, even we, disciples, could array!
Ah, yes, all lofty things attract us, low,
And Christ, His meekness still our stumbling-block!
Here, for all time, there be infallible proofs:
Here, too, whereby to try our days.

                      Who teach
And move men's hearts with words, all orators,
Perceive thoughts of their listeners: Jesus, too,
Followed His audience; proverb in their mind,
A mocking proverb, hindered word of God:—
"Who speaketh of Himself, truth speaks He not;—"
With meekness that amazes, He accepts
Condition thus laid down—sure, not for Him!—
He throws His lot in with us and confirms
Wise adage of the people—He, alone,
Free from the vanity that strives and cries,
Exalts our poor possessions and our parts!
But Christ accepts the rule, brings evidence
As man before his judges saith, "Another
Bears witness of me and His witness true:"
And every man knew in his heart the truth
Of witness borne of God.

                   "To John ye sent,
And he of the truth bare witness. Wist ye not
How that he said, "Behold the Lamb of God?"
I've seen, and know, that this, the Son of God?"
This witnessing of John, how dear to Christ,
A cherished recollection! *Our* poor words
Of love and loyalty, keeps He them in mind?

Why condescends our Master thus to show
The mysteries of Very God to men,

To unbelieving Jews? Not so would we:
His argument He works out point by point,
So, if a man deny, he lies to himself:
We, haughty, scorn such meekness: Let them be!
Purpose He had; by all means, He would save!
So, works, authority and witnesses
Are cited all in turn "*that ye be saved.*"
"John was a lamp that burned and shined in the night,
"And for a season ye rejoiced in light
"For ye were willing: fire of God in him
"Quickened your deadness for a little while!"
Another witness calls He, His own works,—
(Who went about doing good): ah, what if we
Should summon all our work to count for us,
Our poor, marred, broken, ill-done, tangled work,
When good works Thou prepared for us to do!

Once more: "The Scriptures search ye,—these are they
"Which, line on line, tell out the history
"Of Jesus, Virgin-born, of men denied,
"Acknowledged of the Father, glorified.
"Of these things law and prophets testify,
"And yet ye will not unto Me draw nigh!"
(Unwilling *wills*—'tis these deny the Lord!)
"But, how can ye believe who glory seek,
"Honour and praise, from every man ye meet?
"Man cannot serve two masters: ye would choose
"To bring incense of praise and burn it there
"Where self is worshipped; glory I take not
"From men; nor popularity nor power
"At your hands seek I. In My Father's name
"I come, and ye receive Me not: who comes
"In his own name, him joyful ye receive:
"Whoso pretends to genius, learning, skill,
"For his own honour, cordial kindness waits:

"Who doth service for the Father's sake,
"Scant recognition, his! But, I know you;
"The love of God, it is not in your hearts!
"The law of Moses would ye choose indeed
"To guide and rule your lives? Blind, blind are ye!
"Believing Moses, Me ye would believe
"Because he wrote of Me: that very Law
"Ye praise, believe ye as ye please, no more!"

With this last condemnation Christ concludes
That awful charge of awful moment against the Jews:
We, are we guiltless? Do we pick and choose,
Reject or consecrate, as pleaseth us?
"Behaviour, speech, why, these are under law:
"But a man's thoughts, beliefs, he chooses free;
"Nor subject, these, to law of man or God!"
Yet these, the very man: doth God take count
Of unconsidered things of act or speech
Nor heed that spring within whence these take rise?
Thy Jews condemned, grant us, good Lord, to heed!

XXI

JESUS WALKS IN THE CORNFIELDS

IT was a Sabbath still and fair;
The cries of birds and beasts were prayer;
Sweet odours floating on the air
        Ascended straight to God.

And Jesus through the fields of corn
Went, comforted, that Sabbath morn
For the good fruit the seed had borne—
        Seed formed and reared by God.

And other harvest saw He shine
All golden in the light divine,
Harvest of souls—"for those are Mine"
        All sown and reared by God.

Disciples followed, gay and glad,
For who in harvest time were sad
When, filled her bounteous lap earth had
        With the good gifts of God?

As children, plucked they as they went,
And rubbed the ears in sweet content;
With breath, the chaff abroad they sent,
        And ate the bread of God.

But who be these who know no rest,
Who, wheresoe'er He goes, molest,
Nor ever turn from murderous quest
        Of Him, the Bread of God.

What is amiss in this sweet walk,
This simple joy, this cheerful talk?

How find occasion here to balk
       The purposes of God?

They note disciples rubbing ears
Between their palms; offense appears;
In childlike act their slavish fears
       See broken Law of God.

They hurry past the simple men
To where Christ walks in front, and then,
They heap reproaches once again
       On the meek Son of God.

"See now how thy disciples do
Unlawful act on Sabbath, too,
Both thou and they shall learn to rue
       Offence 'gainst Law of God.

And Jesus answering them, said,
"This Scripture story have ye read,
What David did, for he was led
       To know the mind of God;—

"Anhungered he, and much in need
Of wherewithal his men to feed;
So to the Holy Tent made speed
       And asked for bread of God:

"The shewbread He did take and eat
And gave to those, his warriors fleet,
(In days of Abiathar), meet,
       This bread, for priests of God.

"Nay, priests in temple break the law;
On Sabbath day, they water draw

And offer sacrifice—no flaw
       Find ye in priests of God.

"A greater than your priests is here;
Greater than temple, draweth near,
Speaketh in vain to stone-deaf
       The secret things of God!

"Had ye but known what means this word.
Mercy, not sacrifice, the Lord
Preferreth; this will He reward,
       Ye had not grieved your God.

"How can ye read this law benign—
The Sabbath is a gift divine
To man, that all his days may shine
       In the sweet peace of God?

"For man, the Sabbath, not that he
Should go a bondman, but be free
To walk the fields in holy glee
       And hymn the praise of God.

"Lord of the Sabbath is the Son,
And in His righteous reign, begun
E'en now, all men shall joyfully run
       Together to praise God!

XXII

LAW (THE DISCIPLE)

NO vagrant speck of matter, dream of mind,
Finds being, but it straightway finds a mate,
Calm, waiting to receive it—its own law.

With fascinated eyes men watch the law
Take quiet, sure possession of their lives
Through all the incidents that mark the years.

No change of state so quick, but, ere it work,
The Law of the new state doth rise and come,
With the slow ease of one who takes his own,
To grasp, and hold, and rule its issues all.

Fighting wing'd insects, kicking against pricks,
Is all an attempt t' avert the course of Law.
Or act, or say, or do but think a thought,
And such and such shall surely come to pass,
Inevitable sequent of thy thought.

O agony of ever-narrowing walls,
That closer, closer, hedge in work and thought
And love and all of life, till the poor soul,
Ever more straitened, gasps for space to be!

Ah, glad emancipation, then, to see
The true face of the Law! that Law for us,
Not we for Law exist; that Law is Will;
The present, personal, living Will of God,
Whose every motion is a pulse of love!

In a large place straightway the feet are set;
And all the faculties stretch out and play
In that full inspiration of high air!

Within our ken—yet, "after God's own heart";
With thought of relaxation, lessen'd strain,
We seek the spring of this accepted life;—

A sense of sin, by shame and sorrow measured
Forgiveness, raising a white heat of love,
A mighty trust, born of Almighty help,—
In no dead letter do we find these writ,
For in like characters is spelt the tale
Of life in us, e'en to the fullest word
Of sorrow, love, and hope that gushes out;
For not by measure is the Spirit's work,
And not by meed: but out of His own fulness
Pours He forth, till hearts of common men
Find in the yearnings of the King's great heart
The very power of utterance they crave.

And is there nothing more? Was it for this
That He, tho' David's Lord, is called his Son,
As though some kindred likeness dwelt in each?
When He stood offering to slow hands the key
Wherewith to ope the Law, and none would take,
Have ye not read, He said, how David used
This pass to freedom ye do now reject?

A presence, brushing his garments, fanning
His very cheek, is Law to every man,
Yet to dull souls, a presence unperceived;
Things happening day by day in order due,
Do, to their latest day, but happen still.
Fugitive glimpses flash on other minds
Of order, plan and purpose in their lives

More than they wot of; yet are these soon lost
In hurrying details of things immediate.
Others again, of intellect more quick,
Perceive the incessant action of the Law;
Perceive, but to resist: or some, to bow
With a dull acquiescence, as to that
They have no power to hinder or to help.

But, O, the warmth and depth and breadth and height
Of any soul that comprehends the Law
And comprehending, loves it! That, looking round,
Sees the commandment is exceeding broad!

Looking within, sees it exceeding near,
Exceeding mighty, and exceeding sure!
That, looking up, discerns that Law is God!
Ad rapt in awe and wonder, gazing still
Becomes enamoured of the loveliness,
Fair order, use and goodness, that appear
In all the workings he has learned to know
As going forth of God! Henceforth, for him,
All strife and bitterness have ceased from life:
Submission sweet, he learns his times to take
In daily portions as dealt out to him;
Meekly to bear, and as courageous, act.

Such he whose sympathetic thought discerned
The hidden impulse in Messiah's heart,
The Law within—for he, too, loved the Law:
Not as his Lord, with love strong to fulfil,—
Strong only to adore and sore desire!

A soul tuned to order; will, to wait
The bidding of the Law or e'er it stir;
A mind, that with angelic apprehension
Should grasp the boundless reaches spann'd by Law;

Eyes that should see in all affairs of men
The inevitable sequence, which doth yet
Produce as certain good—for this the Law;
And, scanning the great universe, discern,
In all the goings of God's creatures, lines
That blazon to the worlds His Glorious Name;
Nor yet disdain, as in the old star fable,
To predicate the destinies of men,
Proclaiming Law and Order everywhere:—

Such the large longings of this mighty soul:
'Twas not that he attained: alas, his life,
All marr'd by error, strife, and failure, proved
A sad, submissive forfeit to the Law
He found no strength to keep. Yet not by this,
His wretched rendering of the thought within,
But by that thought itself, the broken oft,
Yet still renewed, true purpose of his soul,
Did the just God interpret the King's life.

"Enlarge my heart, for I thy Law would know!"
By this, his large desire, is he judged,
And so accepted; while more lawful lives,
That compass the desires of smaller souls,
Unpraised are passed by; and he alone,
The man who well approved himself to God!

XXIII

CHRIST RESTORES THE WITHERED HAND

THE LORD of the Sabbath gave for peace,
That tumult, work and strife should cease,
And men to House of God draw near
His Praise to utter, Word to hear:—
Sore, as with irritants, the life
Whose every day is given to strife,
Whose labours no cessation know,
Nor pause, for peace of God to flow;
And Christ, who sought the fields for peace
On Sabbath day, found no release:
As nest of hornets, rash disturbed,
The Jews, enormously perturbed,
Round hands and Head, annoying fly
And sting and tease incessantly.
Again in synagogue He taught,
But they a snare for Him had brought,
Man with a withered hand,—for, sure,
This sufferer would His pity lure!

They watched for moment when Christ saw
The man should cause Him break the Law;
Another accusation, "Lo,
This man is of our Law the foe,"
Was ready on their lips; but He
Spake to their thought immediately;
"Rise and stand forth," said to the man,
Who rose and stood, (his hope began
To stir, for knew he not the name
Of Him who, healing sickness, came?)
He rose and stood before them all
At that commanding instant call.
But not to him the Lord's first word;

A searching crucial question heard
The Jews inimical:—"Destroy
Or save, which is the right employ
For Sabbath as for any day?
Evil or good to do, the way
To keep the Law of God?"—their peace
(Despite wrath's sudden, hot increase),
They held; occurred, no meet reply
To question fraught with destiny;
Another chance is theirs: "What man
That owned a single sheep, nor ran,
Knowing it fallen into pit,
With all his might, to rescue it?"
Still ne'er a word from these, obtuse
Of conscience, who will not deduce
A rule of mercy for their lives:
Once more for their conviction strives
The Lord of grace: "Then how much more,
Is worth a man, than sheep by score?"
Wrath of the Lamb men see that day;
In anger He doth them survey,
Grieved for the hardening of their heart,
Insensible to righteous part
The true man takes when wrong and right
Presented, he must judge by light
Lodged in his breast: "Stretch forth thy hand "--
Poor withered limb! But at command,
He did the thing he could not do,
And, lo, this hand was able, too!
Not joyful were the Pharisees,
But filled with madness and unease;
And all their talk and all their thought—
What mischief might on Him be wrought:
Herodians straightway they sought,
And twofold malice 'gainst Him brought,
For these, concerned for Herod's reign,

Watched His success with jealous pain.
And Christ perceiving all their hate,
Withdrew, so might their rage abate!

XXIV

"HE SHALL NOT STRIVE NOR CRY"

ONCE more to lake Gennesareth He came;
Did fair expanse of water mirroring sky,
Mountains and villages, and ways of men
Engaged in business of this inland sea,
The fisher folk and they on traffic bent,
Did simple things like these solace a Mind
Outworn by conflict? Or, was it that here
Dwelt those disciples whom He held most dear?
He came, and of His coming rumour spread
With suddenness, mysterious, of the East;
Great multitude from Galilee followed Him;
And, sick or sinning, lo, He healed them all!
From Judah, too, they came, a mighty host,
From desert region beyond Jordan, crowds
From Tyre and Sidon, cities of old fame,
And from about the brisk Phoenician coasts,—
In multitudes they came; the Kingdom spreads;
That ripple made by weight of truth cast in
Life's torpid waters, much increased and grew.
Equipped with wings, springs hope in every breast;
See, all men bring their sick, and who have plagues,
And press upon Him so that they may but touch,
And go home whole; they too, possessed of fiends:
All see this day the Son and Servant, One,
And know the Father pleased in His Beloved!
He, strong in power of God, that day declared
To Gentiles gathered from the furthest coasts
How God had given all Judgment to the Son;
Nor need they fear, for He was pitiful,
Wherefore the Father trusted Him to judge!
They knew Him meek, nor heard Him cry aloud
Nor strive for right of His with any man;

No clamant tones of His heard they in street;
Bruised, they knew them strengthened and not broke
By gracious words from His lips; poor smoking flax,
Their smouldering thoughts brake into flame of love:
And all those Gentiles hoped upon His Name!

"Behold my servant, He whom I have chosen;
My beloved in whom well pleased is my soul!
My spirit will I upon him pour out,
And judgment to the Gentiles shall he deal.
He shall not strive, nor cry aloud in the streets;
Neither shall any man hear him cry out.
A bruised reed shall he not break,
And smoking flax shall he not quench,
Till he send forth judgment unto victory.
And in his name shall the Gentiles hope."

XXV

Unrest (The Disciple)

SMALL boon is leisure in these restless days!
Rather we crave that every moment find
Us taxed to weariness of limbs and mind,
Kind weariness, that e'en unrest obeys!
For, ah, how life on our tense spirit weighs
In heavy pauses, for our ease assigned,
When needful occupation lags behind,
And, choosing its own paths, the spirit strays!
Aching and longing, quiv'ring with unrest,
For which the moment fain shows cause and name,—
Friends trust us not enough, or cares infest,
Or our own evil grieves, or wrongs inflame;—
The cause is one; at issue still with life,
The soul seeks ease in cries—its peace, through strife!

XXVI

REST (THE DISCIPLE)

PEACE and good will! glory and peace! sweet peace!
A grateful cadence falls on quiet soul
As liquid plash of oar on waters cool:
And life's long straining and endeavour cease;
From turbulent desire comes release;
And restless thought is under perfect rule,
Sitting, meek scholar, in the Master's school,
In hope that to the meek shall scope increase:--
HE shall not strive nor cry, nor in the street,
For any due of His, shall lift His voice;—
But One among the sons of men is meet
For the mild glory of this praise: Rejoice,
When cries are hush'd in thee, strife at an end,—
The King holds court within—My soul, attend!

BOOK III

THE CHURCH

FOUNDATION AND INSTITUTES

XXVII

THE CHURCH OF CHRIST

THE Founder of our Faith place had reached
Where roads divide, and He must choose His way;
No longer should He go in casual wise
Hither and thither as the cities urged:
Henceforth—though He should walk the plains, and preach
In synagogue on Sabbath days, and heal,—
To do these things no longer His chief care:
From out that nebulous crowd that followed Him,
Changing alway, as clouds in windy sky,
Behoved Him to carve out those solid blocks
Shaped duly and laid truly, should support
An Edifice—wide as the world and high
As heaven; roof held on multitudinous piers;
Arches of fretted beauty; windows, broad
To light the soul, and high for aspiration;
Wide-reaching aisles to gather in all folk;
And lowly door meek pilgrims to admit
Who come, in one long stream adown the years
To kneel before the Altar of the LAMB!
Ah, concept vast, immeasurable thought,
Embracing kings and peoples, all poor souls,
Including ages and each present hour,
Pregnant with health, hope, healing for mankind,—
The Church of Christ!
    But who a dome conceives—
How vast be its proportions, high-pitched, roof;—
His first care, the foundations; these must spread,
Must outline compass of the mighty whole,
Must rest secure and strong to bear the weight
Of the slow-rising pile, to pinnacle—
Fair-lettered word on the blue sky writ up!

His time was come: and, as the architect
Figures on parchment the great pile he means,
So Christ, the Church—in all its breadth and height;
Chapels of curious variety,
Each rich in tracery of human thought;
Buttresses to defy ravage of time,—
Attacks of foes and facile arts of friends
Who fain would mould to meet the passing mood
Of each succeeding age its stubborn build:—
Seeing the whole, with urgency on Him
He pressed the imminent occasion
To give it definite shape by His own act;
Henceforth, to set Himself to work on plan,
Eternal in the heavens, of the Church of God!

Like a wise builder, His foundations first
Must He prepare; and that no block unsound
Should jeopardy the Church to rest on it,
Behold, Christ prays, ere choosing His Twelve Stones!

There is a mountain with two several peaks;
Between the two, a little grassy plain,—
The cradle of the infant Church, men hold,
Though not with certainty; else, surely there,
On that lone mountain, Koroun Hattin,
Memorial high as Babel's tower should rise,
Than Solomon's temple, more magnificent!

Thither came Christ to pray; He clomb the height
Of stone-strewn peak, and saw from summit all
That Galilee He loved. Foreseeing thought—
Embracing Galilee and all the parts
Of Judah, all the countries round about,
Regions remote, and time to time's last verge,—
Saw never anywhere in all the world
But, lo, His Church is there to cherish men!

All night He prayed as no man ever prayed;
To no man were such awful issues shown
As saw the SAVIOUR OF THE WORLD that night;
A world to save through ages of endeavour;
And, all the instrument to be employed,
THE CHURCH, that on the morrow He should found!
(Lord Jesus, give us grace to know our part!)

First, for the Twelve He prayed—each man came forth
And passed before the Saviour; each disclosed
All that was in him to the searching thought
Of Him who is our Judge:—ambition, zeal,
Fiery impatience, generosity, greed,
Love, fortitude, devotion, avarice, hate,—
Were open to Him on that lonely night:
What then? The Master would not choose to raise
Upon cohort of seraphs Church for men;
These know not man—how great he is, how small!
Better were men with men's infirmities
But loyal to their Lord; this, the one test:
For the rest, would He not pray for them and save,
Would teach them day by day and every day,
And train them to the following of His Way!
Did one block yield a hollower sound when tried?
E'en that was fit for use, so it would yield
To mallet, chisel, grinding stone, should shape:
And, lo, beneath the twelve, sustaining all,
Christ and His Cross-Foundation, shapes the whole:
The Master Builder's prayer, as each passed by,—
That his faith fail him not!
      Foundations laid
In thought of Him who edified the Church,
Such institutions, impalpable,
As evermore should sever Church from world,—
Should safeguard weak disciple, be a lamp
His feet should go by, rule to try his thoughts,

And mark him other than all other men
Though punctual rite, broad hem, be not for him,—
These next devised our Founder, evermore
Opening His ear to hear the Father's word—
"Of mine own Self I nothing do"—He saith!
That night of prayer, had one been there to tell
What words Christ spake, what counsels He implored,
What help through all the ages for His Church—
Then might that Church take heart nor fret at all,
Though she were the least among the thousand tribes!

XXVIII

The Calling of the Twelve

WHEN the dawn brake, behold, upon the slopes
Of that lone peak, disciples drawn-aware,
Anticipating, fearful, the unknown,—
That which should happen now the day had dawned:
From crowd of the disciples called He straight
Such as He would—none murmuring to be left:
These stood with open soul before the Judge,
Who, as He looked, applied resolving test,—
Was't love and loyalty in eye of each,
Or simple truth as of a little child,
Capacity for affairs, intelligence
To comprehend the mystery of the Cross,
Was't zeal, or steadfastness, or countenance
Witnessed to eloquent tongue, whose burning words
Should quicken life in thousand longing souls?
We know not: all we know,—from out the crowd
Waiting the judgment of the Son of Man,
Some, He rejected; other some, He chose:
Twelve, whom He named Apostles, called He forth:
(How dear to us occasions when the Son
Useth that earliest privilege of man,—
To name the things that be, and in the name
Express the functions, attributes, of each:
Good, He should surname Simon, Levi, give
That designation to the Twelve, to last
While Time goes on, Eternity evolves:
Every such naming of the Lord, more dear
Than chiefest poet's most melodious lay!)

The Apostles—what their part? To be with Him,
Go where He went, gather the words that fell
From lips divine that so, no fragments lost:

Ah, happy Twelve, to hear all words He spake,
To see Him go, in greatness of His might,
Putting to flight all shapes of human ill!
To learn of Him philosophy benign
Should truth discriminate, error confound,
Offer that only clew to labyrinth
Of time and sense and seeming baffles us,
Till, lost in maze, with wandering wits we stray,—
Say, Sure, there is no God, nor heaven, nor hell,
Nothing is anywhere but what we see,
Know through our senses, choose that it shall be!—
As miser finds where he shall hide his gold,
A secret place, secure, strong to resist
Able to hold 'gainst thief, or who, alloy,
Would mix with precious metal and debase,
So Christ, the Giver, found to lodge His words,
Stronghold of those twelve hearts,- oh, holy trust!

"That they might be with Him;" but, came a time
When He should send them forth to preach, give forth
Of that committed to their keeping, teach
Way of salvation to poor souls that strayed,
And, giving freely, should increase the more!
In earthen vessels lodged He all that wealth
Whose scattering should feed His fainting world!

Hear should they, and should preach; but more, He gave
Of that, inherent in Himself alone,
To them as His substance; they should have
Authority, all devils to cast out—
For, how to preach or teach or help poor souls
At mercy of the evil one, who comes
And takes possession, as men claim their own!
Still goeth he about to claw and tear,
To ravage human souls with bestial lusts;
Prudence, we preach, and temperance, and hope

Of good things of this world for who shall cast
His evil from him and go forth, clean man:
Poor wretch, of what avail? No power he has;
In one Name only can he be set free;
And this Name the Apostles, graced to use
(Else were their preaching vain), Deliverers,
Went forth to captive thralls and set them free!

To hear and hold and treasure up the Word,
To teach and preach and spread abroad the Word,
To deliver captive souls by that great Word,—
To these three offices were consecrate
The Twelve Apostles; all these they fulfilled.
Who were these Twelve—most honoured among men—
Names we revere, on whose word build our faith?
Peter and Andrew, James and John, we know;
Nearest and dearest to their Lord,
Because they loved much and yet were meek:
Simon, unstable, yet a rock, we learned,
Gat new name from his Lord; those other two,
John we call gentle, and his brother James—
Too bold are we—But, see we smile, the Lord?
Doth tender humour for the instant show
In Christ's kind eyes, as, seeing fiery zeal
In the meek brothers, "Boanerges," He
Straight named those Sons of Thunder, gentle saints?
Bartholomew we love, for he, Nathanael;
Glad, we, that modest Levi here to meet
Amongst the chosen Twelve, graced with a name
Dear to all Christian folk, as one of Four
Who for us wrote Evangel of our Lord;
That other James, and Simon, zealot called—
Of sect confounding politics and faith;
Philip and Thomas, he of doubtful mind;
And Judas, son of James, called Thaddeus,
(How bear the name of him betrayed the Lord?)—

These five we scarce know yet; emerge shall each
From the Holy Company as occasion bids:
Remains but Judas—man of Kerioth:—
Lord, seven times seventy Thou bidd'st forgive;
Woulds't Thou bid pardon him betrayed Thee?
Too hard, O Lord, for us, too hard is this!
If pardon must we, Thou, enable us!

XXIX

The Ordination Charge

THEN came He down and stood on level place
(That grassy, flowery plateau 'twixt the peaks)
He stood, the Twelve about Him: limner's art—
Showing the figures of the Chosen Men
In glow of their initiation, meek
As infants brought to Font; the face of Him,
Our source of life and light, shedding on these
The love that had drawn them to that strict embrace
Of common labour for a common end;
Dark background of the mountain, glow from east;—
Had given the Church a constant-springing fount
Of inspiration; had but Luke been there!
Multitudes of disciples gathered were;
Of people from Judea and the coast,
From regions round about on every hand,
Another multitude had come to hear.
They watched Him come, descending from the height,
The glory of His goodness shining out
Resplendent in their dark; they press to touch
If but the hem of His garment, and be healed
Of every ill tormented soul and flesh:
Sea of expectant faces shone in light
Of the fresh morning sun: He sat and taught.

"Ah," say those hapless ones who will not have
In Christ more than man is, can do, may be:
"Here is the religion that we all may hold,
In that so simple Sermon on the Mount,
Setting forth all that is due from man to man
As a wise pagan might—nor less nor more!"
Is it in truth so easy, that sweet law
Of eight-fold blessing on the righteous man?

Not one familiar virtue's in this scheme
Of all beatitudes! Sages had taught
An hundred ways of virtue for a man;
But these—what place for all that emulous pride
Urges a man to distance all the rest
In honour, virtue, learning, fair renown?
"Such teaching is subversive, him exalts
Whom men despise; condemns whom all men praise!"
"Behold, I make all new;" the Master saith;
And this low western Portal of His Church—
With arches eight, all low and narrow ways,—
No easy, ample pilgrim struggles through!

XXX

BLESSED ARE YE POOR

THE Lord spake:—
        "Blest are ye poor!"
The happy man is not elate
With riches, honour, or estate:
When all goes well, behold him mild
And simple as a little child.
All things against him, he is blest,
His heart in simpleness at rest,
Nor vexes heaven with the cry,
"O what unhappy wretch am I!"
The humble man hath lowly ways;
As little child he takes his days:
Not well or ill thinks of himself;
Eluding that insistent elf,
Not of himself he thinks at all;
So, heaven and earth are at his call!
Vicegerent of God's Kingdom, he
Dispenseth bounties royally!
With humble plant, see you, he's girt,
Which pluckt, springs up again unhurt!*
*The rush wherewith Virgil girded Dante
To the disciples turned the Lord,
And, looking on them, spake the word,—
        "Blest are ye poor!"
About the Twelve, know one thing more,—
Poor men were they in heart and store.
"Woe to you rich, for, understand,
All ye may hope is in your hand!"

XXXI

BLESSED ARE YE THAT HUNGER AND THIRST

THE Master said:—
"Blest are ye hungry;"—ye who taste
How dully hours and years may waste
In talk insipid, pleasures stale,
New scenes, employs of small avail
To cure distemper of the heart
That hath not found its worthy part:—

Blest are ye hungry—ye that tread
A heavy way, grey skies o'erhead,
Lonely in long procession, sad,
Of folk whose brows are rarely glad;
Who toil and fret for daily bread,
And, getting that, are scantly fed:—

Blest are ye hungry—poet souls,
Whom tender hue, bird lilt, consoles;
Who yet, an-hungered in our ways,
Go, lacking, to sustain the days,
That purpose high, that generous aim,
Shall all a man's endeavour claim:—

Ye who are sated, and not fed,—
Ye dreary whom yet none has led
In pleasant ways,—ye ardent wills
Whom earth nor solaces nor fills,—
Come ye, come all! There's bread to spare,
Delicious draught for you to share!

Know we to name the things we need,
Seek bread of God our soul to feed,
Water of life to satisfy,—

Who hears the ravens when they cry
Hath promised we, too, shall be filled,
Our cravings eased, our crying, stilled!

"Blessed *ye* hungry," saith the Lord
To those disciples heard His word:—
The Twelve, an-hungered, knew their need,
And wait as birds on scattered seed;
Peck at the Word and take their fill
As greedy fowl with eager bill!

XXXII

"Blessed are ye that mourn"

And spake the Lord
        "Blest, ye that mourn!
Ye, sorrowful, that sadly go
Contrite for all your nation's Woe;
Know, every vice of rich and poor;
Your people's sin, lies at your door!
Well may'st cast ashes on thy head
Who seldom hath admonished
Or taught or helped, or given thy life
To stop the fratricidal strife
Brother from brother rends apart,
In village home, in city mart!
No separate place for thy poor soul,
Thine is the Wrong infects the whole!
Well may'st thou weep (and work the while),
For lust and ravage, which defile
God's chosen place, a people's heart
Erst for His glory set apart!
But Weep no more; glad, go thou forth;
These Augaean stables of the earth
Shall yield to Cleansing Arm, not thine,
But thine, to share in task divine
Who knows power with him well may laugh
How poor the grain, how much the chaff
In that poor ear of effort grown
From seed of Word so freely sown!

To the disciples said the Lord,
Of certain hope, a joyful word;
        "Blest, *ye* that mourn!
The Twelve their secret heart disclose;
Another grace in *them* he knows

Who tries them by the word of God!
Not theirs, insensible as clod,
Their Israel's woes to disregard
Nor grieve at chastisements, full hard
For people of Jehovah's land
To bear at alien nation's hand!
   Blest, ye that mourn
For you that laugh and sing to-day,
Nor heed at all your people's smart,
Nor in their anguish claim your part
Your woe shall tarry not, nor stay!

XXXIII

OF PERSECUTIONS

HOW piteous for a mother to behold
Her daughter faint and worn with nursing cares,
Borne for the mother who would fain bear all!
Piteous for father, strong young son to see
Out-wrought with labour, all for care of him!
But, ah, how piteous to the heart of Christ,
All woes should fall upon the Chosen Twelve!
The "Everlasting Father" reached out arms
Of comforting: "Rejoice, that day," saith He,
"When men shall persecute you, drive you forth
"From synagogue, outcast from kith and kin,
"Reproached and buffeted, and all for Me!
"Rejoice when those days come and leap for joy!
"Thus fared it with the prophets; so are ye
"Placed on the roll of them went forth to war
"For God against the nations, fear not ye;
"He that is for you's greater than they all;
"And He hath secret ways of solacing
"Who suffer for His Name; in heaven and now
"Is your reward when these things come to pass;
"In stonings, martyrdoms, scourgings and fears,
"The joy of God shall as in fiery car
"Bear you above all malice of the world;
"Rejoice that day, and be exceeding glad!
"But, do men praise you, flatter to your face,
"Seek ye as oracles, reward in hand,
"Pour world's prosperity upon your head
"As ointment sweet of savour? Woe to you!
"False prophets thus their fathers cherished;
"When all goes well with you, be ye afraid!"
The Twelve heard, fearful,—and all their present thought,

Messiah's kingdom they were called to spread;
If need were, die for; follow Him through all!

XXXIV

ORDER OF THE DAY

THE Lord taught them, saying:
No man counts salt itself a thing of worth,
Nor numbers, amongst treasures of the earth;
But, salt away, how vapid is our meat!
Lacking his salt, who would persist to eat?

Ye, Twelve, small handful in the a mighty whole,
Salt of the earth are ye, and every soul
Shall savour life as ye shall make it good,
Or, turn disgusted from insipid food.

But, take ye heed, its savour salt may lose,
And he who tastes, offended, shall refuse;
"Cast out the worthless thing," saith he, "tis waste,
"False promised good, deceitful to the taste!"

The world immense in darkness lieth quite,
And ye, poor Twelve, its single glimmering light;
All that ye are stands clear revealed to men,
As city set on hill towers o'er the plain.

A bushel-measure makes a useful stand
For lamp, that who would work may have at hand;
On all within the house it shineth free;
But, light 'neath o'erturned measure, who shall see?

A lamp must shine; e'en so ye must give light;
Men seeing all ye do, must judge it right;
Good works done simply (as a lamp doth shine),
Men recognise as wrought through grace divine.

Think ye I came to make an easier lot
For them should follow Me, the Law forgot;
Its binding precepts, things of small concern
If one from Moses to My Kingdom turn?

To keep the Law, not to destroy, I came!
Nor shall one least commandment, without blame
By him be broken who is called by Me
To manifest God's light that men may see.

The Pharisees, think ye, are over strait;
But whoso enters at the Kingdom's gate,
Not less, but greater righteousness must show;
In straiter ways must rule his feet to go!

XXXV

FURTHER ORDERS

AND He spake:—
Behold the day's instruction—see how strait!
No outlet find ye here for natural hate:
Who love you not, e'en they your love must share,
And those who hate, be objects of your care.

Curse they? Bless ye. Offend they? Ye must pray;
Solicit God to show them worthier way:
Smite they in malice unoffending cheek?
Then turn the other in rebuking meek.

What if they take thy cloak and leave thee cold?
Offer thy coat to him hath been so bold;
Well, if thy kindness open that man's eyes
To see the blessedness of sacrifice!

Not thy own rights or wrongs—thy brother's part
In that must urge itself upon thine heart;
That he offends, not that thou suffer loss,—
In this the anguish of a brother's cross.

I send you forth, the brothers of all men;
From he would take thy goods, ask not again;
Doth any beg of thee? Then freely give;
As brothers loving brothers, shall ye live.

And doth your natural heart cry out in pain,
That smitten, grieved, ye needs must grieve again?
I tell you, nay; what ye would have men do
To you, the rule your conduct must pursue.

Who thanks a man for loving his own friends,
For gifts to those who, giving, make amends?
For lending to the man, lends him again?
E'en sinners so much common grace attain.

But ye go forth to show the Father's Name,
Never despairing, lending; still the same
Though they you bless turn on you but to curse—
Yet, love alway, through better as through worse.

'Tis thus your Father loves; and ye must show
The pattern of His Kindness as ye go;
The unthankful, evil, at His hand receive;
And these shall ye be ready to relieve.

Lo, sons of the Most High, shall ye go forth
To witness of Him to His thankless earth;
Would ye, reward? To be like God, the best
Of all those gifts with which His sons are blest.

Be merciful as He, nor think hard things
Of him who wrongs thee; or, occasion brings
Against the Church: nay, judge not thou his case;
For, what were thy behaviour in his place?

E'en as it is, be sure he hath no plea
To make to God the Father against thee:
Who judgeth men, into God's judgment comes;
Who blames another, his own reckoning sums!

Give, and men give to thee; forgive, they're kind;
Release, and no man hastens thee to bind;
The measure that thou met'st is thine again,—
Pressed down, heaped up, and running o'er, the grain.

In heaven is thy reward, and it is great;
Wide fiefs within the kingdom, thine estate;
And men make haste to fill the measure up—
To overflow with bounties thy full cup.

XXXVI

THE NURSERY (THE DISCIPLE)

THE babes are left in charge of elder child;
    The mother, to and fro, sees all goes well,
    Nor looks that any of another tell—
She sees if they be tranquil, good and mild:—

And every place where men together come,
    The home, the prison, school, the royal court,
    Big Factory, college, camp, or ship, or fort,
Now, what is each but just a cottage room—

The babies left in charge of elder child?
    The Father of us all goes to an fro;
    Needs none to tell Him how his matters go:
He knows the children turbulent and wild,—

But ever saith He to the elder child,
    He, scarce less silly than the babes, his care,—
    "Lest you should hurt the little ones, beware,
"For very kind must be the elder child!"

"But, Father, see the babes, how silly, they!
    "They pluck out hair, and scream and vex my heart,
    "They spoil my toys, nor, in my games take part!"
The Father hears his plaint, and yet doth say,
"Now, very kind must be the elder child!"

"Father, thou knowest best; and well for me,
    "For Thy sake to endure small-tyrant ways;
    "I serve, not seeking love or thanks or praise;
"But sure, their reckless wrong displeaseth Thee?"

"My child, hast yet to learn the secret sure
 "Of loving silly sheep for whom I died!
 "Loving with love that will not be denied;
"For their sake, not for Mine, shalt thou endure!

"Think on my servant Moses, his great love;
 "How with firm hand he ruled; he prayed, he taught;
 "And when God's anger 'gainst the people wrought,
"Cried, 'Blot me, also, from Thy book above!'

"Know'st thou the brother-secret, all is learned;
 "Thou giv'st thy coat, thy cloak, thy strength, thy hope;
 "Thou askest nought but for their service, scope;—
 "For them, would'st give thy body to be burned!
  "This is to love, as I have loved thee,
  "To see in the unlovely, only Me."

XXXVII

Six Parables

THE Lord spake:—
Did'st ever see a blind man take the hand
Of brother blind man, bid him go or stand?
Full soon the two in wayside ditch would roll.
And shall a blind man see to lead the soul.
Of his blind brother to the things he ought?—
Who teacheth other must himself be taught.

Fret ye, My children, at a heavy rede?
Who follows master lets his master lead,
Nor would he go before or sit above;
So grows he perfect in his master's love;
If I, your Master, learn and suffer long,
Is't yours to sit at ease, and think no wrong?

Ye follow Me, ye say, but bid Me note
In thy poor brother's eye an alien mote;
Nay, 'tis a little thing; think of thine own,
A monstrous beam is there; when that is gone,
Then wilt thou see to clear thy brother's sight
Of every hindrance shuts him from the light.
Thou hypocrite, would'st magnify the blame
Thy brother bears,—so dost reveal thy shame!

Tree planted in the garden of the Lord,
Take heed that good, the fruit thou dost afford;
For every tree by its own fruit is known;
Thorns bear not figs, nor bramble, grapes adorn:
Word, thought, and act, each tree yields of its kind,—
Good, from the good, ill, from the evil mind.

Or, keeps a man a treasure to impart
To guests that come to him from field or mart?
Well fareth the man's guest if he be good—
Refreshing vintage and delicious food!
But if the man be evil, barren fare
Shall spread his scanty table, victuals spare:
The heart, that closet whence man brings his store;
Of his abundance doth he freely pour:
Good words to whosoe'er brings ear to hear,
If heart be good; if that be insincere,
A miser's shallow store, his mouth affords
Of poor and mean, of base, malicious words.

Two men bethought them each a house to build
Abutting on a river; one man willed
His dwelling on the rock to edify;
And, ere he raised a homestead broad and high,
Laboured at the foundations, digging deep
In the hard rock while idle men went, sleep;
Trench in the rock due hollowed, safe and sure
Laid he foundations there, to rest secure
Whatever violence should put to proof:
Careful, he raised the walls and laid the roof:
And, all things done, he went at ease to dwell,
Glad in reward of him who doeth well!
The summer sun dissolved the mountain snows;
Behold, the river in a flood uprose,
And brake against that house with frantic force!
The inmate sat secure; he knew no worse
Than violent beating of the turbulent wave
Should damage him and his; proved strength should save—
Foundations laid secure and solid walls—
From raging tempest, strongest heart appals'
His neighbour, zealous, too, a house to raise,
By rapid building won men's idle praise;
The river's sandy bank afforded site;

Foundations dug he none, but quick, upright,
His walls he raised, his roof laid on space,
And, dwelling under cover, laughed in face
Of that slow man who took such heavy pains.
But see, the river swelleth with the rains:
The lapping water urges 'neath the wall,
The house is filled and shaking to its fall;
The winds and waves soon lay it with the ground,—
And great the ruin of that house is found!
Would'st know the meaning of the simple tale?
There be who hear My word without avail;
Well-pleased, they listen as to pleasant song,
And idly reckon them My friend among.
"Lord, Lord;" they cry, nor do the thing I say;
But, by life's swelling river, careless play
At building house of ease, no stronger found
Than baby-castle raised on sandy ground!
The swelling river, turbulent and strong,
Beats down and carries that poor house along;
Or doubts, or loss, or grief, or passing days,
Destroy the fabric of men's ready praise;
And the poor man who built it, lost is he,
Not having known to rest the whole on ME.
That other man—he heard and pondered deep,
Resolved each word within his heart to keep;
Laboured until, through words and acts of Mine,
Pondering, discerned he the Truth divine;
Upon that Rock *I am*, his house he raised;
And henceforth, no more fearful nor amazed,
How wild be error's, awful, passion's might--
At ease dwells he in house he builded right!

XXXVIII

THE SERMON ON THE MOUNT

THUS spake Christ; first, to those most near His heart,—
Disciples, should in all His work have part:
Close gathered they about Him, where the plain
In skirt of mountain merges:—How attain
To knowledge of the sayings, every day
Must see them practise as they tread the Way?

Now, Jesus raised His eyes and saw the crowd
Pressing to hear the Word; but not allowed
For multitude of followers surging near;
So clomb He up the Mount that all might hear:—

"Blessed are the poor, for theirs the kingdom is;
Blessed are the mourners; they shall enter bliss
Blessed are the meek. What shall they have of Me?
The earth they did not seek for, theirs in fee!
Blessed are the hungry souls; they shall be filled;
Their thirst be satisfied; their craving stilled.
Blessed are the merciful, whose tender art
Knows how to make their own a brother's part;
Though they be sinners, mercy at My hand
Claim they; because they mercy understand.
Blessed are the pure in heart; for them the sight
Isaiah saw—God throned in His might!
Blessed are they who heal up strife; theirs, a new name,—
Them, sons of God, the angel-hosts acclaim!
Blessed ye, when persecuted for My sake;
Kingdom of heaven, then, rise up and take!

XXXIX

AT SCHOOL (THE DISCIPLE)

SAVIOUR! Thou will'st me poor,—
   Haughty and rich am I;
In self-dependence rich,
   Presuming, hard and high: —
Faith, looking on the coming years, doth see
Dark faults, sore failures, let to humble me.—
   Thy will be done!

A mourner must I be:
   And holy messengers
Oft have Thy presence left
   To bring me blessed tears:
Too soon they fail, and sin's hot breath sweeps by:
Then wilt Thou take the spot, and show it me
Till, weeping, fain I turn to hide in Thee:
   Thy will be done!

Meek wouldst Thou have Thy child:—
   How little can I bear!
How seldom wait for Thee,
   Quiet within Thy care!
Tho' through provokings, teach me to endure;
Bid errors make me of myself less sure:
   Thy will be done!

A hungering, thirsting one
   Must Thy disciple be:
And I so full! grown fat
   On Thy gifts, leaving Thee!
But Thou wilt teach me want, or take away
All lesser food, till Thou, my only stay!
   Thy will be done!

Merciful as Thou art!
   O, how harsh judgments rise!
O this censorious tongue,
    Evil discerning eyes!—
Yet His sweet mercy will my King impart,
If by no other way, e'en through the smart
Of pity withheld in my extremities:
   Thy will be done!

Pure, e'en in Thy pure eyes!
   Single and free from guile;
O when shall these vain thoughts
   Pure rising, meet Thy smile?
E'en this though Christ is mine; though it should be
That first, through purging fires, Thou go with me.
   Thy will be done!

Ruled by the Prince of Peace.
   How far from this my state;
Oft striving for my own,
   Exacting, harsh, irate!
No peace is found in me; but Thou wilt come
And make this chafing bosom Thy sweet home:—
   Thy will be done!

Thus I abide His time;
   For hath the King not sworn
That all these shall be mine,
   And will He not perform?
If tender ways shall serve, such wilt Thou use,—
But smite, if need be; I would not refuse.
   Thy will be done!

XL

THE OLD RULE AND THE NEW:
OF LOVE AND HATE

THE Lord said:—
"Thou shalt not kill," was spoken in old time;
        And whoso kills shall be to judgment brought:
        I say to you that each resentful thought,
Harboured against thy brother, is a crime.

Shall bring thy soul to judgment; have a care
        How thou lett'st out thy wrath in words of scorn
        Intemperate, in pride and fury born;
Of judgment, council, fire of hell, beware!

"A word," thou sayst, "is but a thing of breath,
        A man on heated impulse cries 'Thou fool,'
        Would fain recall the slight when he is cool—
For so small trespass is he worthy death?"

Nay, thou may'st call him "Raca," any name,
        Spoken in kind rebuke, or anger just,
        Or play of love; who speaks in sudden lust
Of rage would kill, his word takes deadly aim.

Nor need he speak; each surging vengeful thought,
        To Him with whom ye have to do, is plain;
        As stab of dagger, too, the murderous pain
Of hate which yet no harm to flesh hath wrought.

Not what ye do, but what, in secret, feel,
        Condemns or justifies before your Lord:
        So leave your offering; if some hasty word
Rankle in brother's heart, make haste to heal;

Then, to Mine altar come with praise and prayer:
> Agree with him who hath against thee aught,
> Lest, quick, it come to pass that thou be brought
Before My judgment seat offence to bear:—

I say to you, the man who nurses hate
> Must adversary seek with acts of love—
> Gentle as lamb, tender as nesting dove—
Lest reconcilement come for him too late!

This is the whole law—who loves cannot offend;
> Nor hurt his brother's body, wound his heart;
> Let every man with thee have brother's part,
And whoso grieves thee, cherish as thy friend.

XLI

OF CHASTITY

AND the Lord spake:—
Know thou thy body, pure, a Holy Place
      For incense of thy prayer;
      An altar, where
Continual sacrifice is offered up;
Where every day thou spill'st oblation's cup
Of filial praise before the Father's face!

But what these fumes of horrid thoughts, impure,
      A woman's face hath stirred,—
      A soft air, heard,
A tale of love and lust hath conjured quick—
Till prayer and praise, My service, turn thee sick?
Though nothing hast thou done, thy sin is sure:

'Tis not what a man does, but what he thinks,
      Emotions he lets rise
      When eyes meet eyes,
Hand toucheth hand, although lips silent be,—
These be the spells unchaste divide from Me;
For can man worship God the while he sinks,

Faint with desire, before an alien shrine?
      Adultery of the heart,
      An easy part
That risks not penalty before the law,
A sin insidious, a man may draw
To lose his soul and body, which be Mine.

Then guard thee when thou walkest in the street,
      Nor see lewd play, or look,
      Nor read loose book;

Nay, if thine eye offend thee pluck it out,—
Cast it away, nor join the unclean rout
Of them, for body's lust would hell fire meet.

Is't thy right hand would thee to stumble make,
        With thrilling touch and grasp,
        Hot passion's clasp?
Nay, cut it off, and never heed the pain;
To lose thy several members were thy gain,
So, fire of lust not in thy body wake!

Nor think to bring desire within the law,
        By writing out a bill
        That shall make nil
Thy marriage with the wife who shares thy home;
If in her place another woman come,
In lust and sin ye two together draw.

Nay, keep thy soul a garden of the Lord,
        Where *I* may walk at eve,
        Nor e'er perceive
The heavy odour of an unchaste thought—
The turbulence of nerves and blood is wrought—
But quiet keep thee, that thou hear My word!

XLII

OF GUARDED SPEECH

AND spake the Lord:—
They of old time forbade a man to swear,
Save he, to keep his oath 'fore God, had care:
Swear not at all, I bid; there is no place
In universe thou see'st where oath finds grace:

Swear not by heaven; it is the throne of God;
Nor by the earth; it is the lowly sod
Whereon doth rest the feet of the Great King;
Jerusalem, His city; darest thou bring

'Gainst that is His, offense of foolish oath?
To swear by thine own head shouldst thou be loth,
That, too, belongs to God; nor canst thou make
One hair or white or black for any sake.

But thou, like duteous son, must sacred keep
Thy father's wealth; nor rudely overleap
Restrictions He hath laid on all that good
With generous hand He hath bestowed.

Assault not with rude words His holy Name,
But humble, gracious, thy true sonship claim;
Honour His name, His Word, the things that bear,
In countless characters, signs of His care!

Why offer confirmation of thy word?
All men have test to try the truth when heard
While they let lies deceive, the truth they know,
And bear an inward witness—"it is so."

If, then, ye cannot prove the words ye say,
Keep ye to simple speech,—plain yea, or nay;
The man who hears, his to discern the right;
Thy flow of words will not make darkness light.

Asseveration is the way of fools;
And who his speech by God's high ordering rules
Will shrink from oath for confirmation meant,
Nor will, to hear men's blasphemies, consent.

Bethink thee: words thou speak'st are not thine own;
Nor aught thou see'st is for thee alone;
Bethink thee: words are things; with violence used,
They hurt, and injure, as the flesh is bruised

By missile rude. Speak soft, as at king's court,—
No word so low, but God hears the report;
Speak simple truth, and who receives thy word,
The very word of God through thee hath heard.

XLIII

"BE YE PERFECT"

AND still the people listened, Christ spake on:
The sun rose high in heaven, the sun declined,
And still the people heard, the Master spake;—
Till all these institutes which should constrain,
Instruct, inspire His Church were set forth plain.
He spake—and it was said: no further word
Might evermore be added to the Law,—
New Law of Christian Life, proclaimed He then.
Association, with no personal aim,—
Hope of advancement, wealth, success or praise,—
He framed that day, and gave it all its laws:
What then in place of all that moves a man,
Stirs him to great endeavour for high praise?
Just love, no more; love, for the Father's sake,
Should keep their lights aburning before men,
Savour of holiness in all their ways,
Who reckoned them disciples: Love should rule
In straitest discipline their thoughts, words, acts,—
No easy-going liberty for them!
Love for their fellows should endure the worst—
Endure and serve, the order of the day.
Small wonder if with quaking heart they heard—
The Twelve and those about them—counsels, asked
Perfection in who follow! Who were they?
Fishers and folk no better than the rest—
How should they, sudden, lead the perfect life
Fit only for God's angels? It is hard.

But never thought but finds its way to Him
Who knows the stuff we're made of; did He abate,—
Pity their imperfection, let them down
To easy living in the common way?

Nay, as rider quickens flagging horse,
Christ spurr'd to high endeavour. "Perfect, ye
"Shall as your Father be, which is in heaven!
"Think how His sun doth rise day after day
"On good and ill alike, How falls His rain
"On just man and unjust! E'en so shall ye
"Give and forgive, be merciful and mild,
"Water the thankless with unsparing wealth
"Of love and hope, of service and kind ways."

Well, Lord, for them who heard Thy blessed voice
To rise to Thy demand! But what for us,
Poor souls, who yet Thy true disciples be,
Who nought in heaven have but only Thee,
Nor compare aught on earth! Yet never day
But we do fail to show the light Thou gav'st,
Lose savour of Thy word, resent and hate,
Indulge our flesh and lie and Thee forswear!
What hope for us in whom is no good thing?

Not perfect shall we go, gods were we else:
But once a day, or twice, may it not be,
Loving and meek and humble, stand we forth
If but an instant, perfect before God!
And in that instant's vision strong, we go
A step or two; then fall and weep and pray,—
Lord, guide once more our steps into the WAY!

XLIV

OF ALMS

BUT there is more to say; not yet her way
The Church might find, through all the days to come,
By light of luminous words the Master spake:
Her prayers, her alms, her fastings, anxious cares
For little matter of the daily life—
What rule to follow? Do as the Jews?

The Lord spake:—
Your light shall shine 'fore men, ye know not how;
No goodness shall ye do that it be seen.
There be who give an alms away
Sound out a trumpet, give in a public place,
And idle men praise them who bid for praise;
Glory these men get from men, nor seek from God.
But wilt thou give an alms? Thy heart is sore
For that thy brother lacks what thou hast got;
Thou wilt not shame him by an open boon,
Wilt scarce to thine own self revel thine act,
And blush to think upon it; who art thou,
What better than the brother needs thy help?
So taking heed to find a quiet place
With bashful kindness offerest thou thy gift,
And he takes brother's love as well as meat,—
Thus his lean heart is nourished, God is pleased.

XLV

OF PRAYER

THY prayers—a secret commerce with thy God—
In closet with closed doors, shalt offer up:
What man in public makes his vows to her
He chooseth for his wife? Less sacred these,
Than vows thou mak'st to God, less intimate:
Who but the Father knows thy heart's whole pain,
Its joy, desire, its aspirations, grief,—
And these thou bring'st to God in secret prayer:
Poor soul, how lonely wert thou if were none
Whom thou couldst seek in secret and tell all
How, for a day, couldst thou support a life
Not breathing instantly that air divine
Thou reachest in thy closet with closed doors?
As a man climbs a mountain for free air,
So risest thou to spirit-altitudes
While low thou kneelest at thy Father's feet,
And show'st Him all thy sorrow, sin and shame,
And love that will not leave Him till He bless!
Behold, the thing thou pray'st for thou hast got -
For never absent is the hearing Ear,
Never grown cold the Father's tenderness,
And, all His child doth ask for, God doth give
Quick as the thunder follows lightning flash!
Who kneeleth on his knees, he summons God
To hear and answer that thing he would say:
Then wilt thou let thy errant thoughts roam here
Roam there, on thousand idle quests, the while
Thou fill'st the pause by speaking vainly much?
Prepared be thy petitions, shortly said,
In reverent assurance that He knows,
Thy Father, what thou need'st or e'er thou ask,
But chooseth that His children ask of Him

Vain repetitions use not, as do they
Who know not God and send their prayers aloft
In vague uncertain hope they may find place,
And all the more that they do reiterate.
So speaks not he to whom a King gives ear;
Few words and apposite he fain would say
In moment of his audience, lest the King
He weary with his verbiage. Is God less?
Come, I will show ye how ye ought to pray:—

XLVI

"OUR FATHER"

HALLOW in my vain heart Thy holy Name,
Hallow in my dear home Thy tender Name,
Hallow in all Thy church Thy blessed Name,
Hallow throughout the world Thy mighty Name,
    Our Father!

Within my rebel heart rule Thou, my King,
Over my wilful-dear, rule Thou, their King,
More constant, may Thy Church serve Thee, her King
And grant that all the nations know their King,
    Our Father!

Ah Lord, my will is stubborn, do Thy will!
May they whom I hold dear adore Thy will,
In all Thy holy Church work Thou Thy will,
And bid the peoples haste to do Thy will,
    Our Father!

Give all of us this day our daily bread,
The starving multitudes their daily bread,
Heart-hungry and mind-hungry, give us bread,
To us who hunger for Thee, give our bread,
    Our Father!

My Father, I have sinned! Do thou forgive,
Thy church, Thy people, sin, do Thou forgive,
They sin who know Thee not, good Lord, forgive,
And teach us, sinful, that we too, forgive,
    Our Father!

Temptation is at hand, deliver us!
We of this household pray, deliver us!

For all Thy church entreat, deliver us,
And for all men beseech, deliver us,
                    Our Father!

Our Father, hear Thy children's prayer,
Keep us this day within Thy care!
                    AMEN.

Thus, boldly, bade the Lord His people pray,
For God, our Father, will not say us nay;
Pray for ourselves, our dear ones, all mankind,—
We all are children to the Father's mind:
For, our profoundest need, God's grace to share—
His Name, His Will, His Kingdom, our first care;
Then, free, we ask for our immediate needs,
Meat, pardon, guidance; Who His children feeds
Will give, forgive, and guard us from our foes:
One sole condition doth the Lord impose;
"Forgiven, would'st thou be?" Remit his score,
Nor let thy brother's trespass vex thee more!

XLVII

OF FASTING

AND then, of fasting spake the Son of man,
Who knows the needs of flesh: "Art sorry, thou,
Afflicted for the sins thou dost commit,
Afflicted for thy nation's many sins,
Afflicted for calamity befalls
The people thou art one with; grievest most
For that Thy God doth turn away His face
And prayer falls flat—word said without response?
Doth meat offend, should satisfy thy flesh,
So sore do flesh and spirit strive in thee?
'Tis well that thou should'st fast and weep and pray,
Take hold upon Him, not to let Him go
Unless He bless thee with the morning light!
But these, the secret things thou hast with God!
Disclosed to men, breathed on with common breath—
'Tis as the Holiest were trod by feet
Not consecrate with Me. So, smiling, go.
And cheerful among men as though no weight
Pressed heavy on thy spirit. God will cheer
The sorrow God doth send—to live upon.
The secret of His chidings dare disclose,—
Men's foolish praise, and pity, thy reward;
Not recompense that cometh from the Lord!

XLVIII

OF BEING ANXIOUS

AND spake the Lord:—
"All men desire treasure, that the heart,
Vexed by things contrary, may sudden dart
And steal an instant's look at that lies by,
Or wife, or child, or work, ambition high;—
In contemplation of his treasure, strong;
The man goes forth to strive his peers among.
But men there be who cherish trivial joys,
Mere things that money buys and rust destroys,
And moth devours, reducing to vile dust;
Or place, the worldly covet, for they must,
Not knowing all appointments held for ME.
Choose well, My servant, what thy treasure be,
For where thou lay'st thy holdings—there thy heart,
Will, mind and purpose, effort, every part:—
Shall all thou art be spent on things of earth?
But, fear not, son; Thy Father knows thy birth,
The cravings of thy nature for the best;
With Me are laid up treasures at thy hest—
Love, joy, and praise, tranquillity and power;
Sweet graces to illumine every hour
Of thy dark pilgrimage; come, bank with ME,
And where thy treasure is thy heart shall be!"

XLIX

OF THE SINGLE EYE

THE Lord spake on:—
Thou 'plainest,—How to know what I shall choose!
Things of this world beguile me and confuse;
I gather worthless treasures in my hand,—
How can I lay these up at Thy command?

My son, first teach thyself to think aright;
The things so dazzled thee, 'twas not their light
But an illusive brilliance cast by thee;
The eye itself brings light by which to see.

See to it that thou keep the single eye;
That eye, in all the star-bespangled sky,
Sees but one Sun of righteousness, nor bends
To that mock lustre its own shining lends.

Seek not, thy glory, power, advancement, praise,—
Or how shall ardent eye to heaven raise?
But look on Him thou servest, so thy frame
With guiding light of love shall be aflame!

Dark is the body, with the evil eye,
As house which doth the light of day deny;
But light and giving light, the eye that sees—
Secure, the seeing man and goes with ease.

L

OF SERVING GOD AND MAMMON

NOT lawful, then, for thee two lords to serve;
To one or other must thou ever swerve
With love and loyalty; the other, hate;
And thy forced service hour by hour abate:

Thou would'st serve Mammon? Thou shalt be his thrall;
Thy love, thy reverence, duty—he claims all!
How to get more, what thou hast got, display,
The first, last, thought of every sordid day!

Would'st thou serve Me? What then to thee his lures?
Or much, or little, thy content ensures:
Thine aims are other than thy little gains;
Toward Me, thy desire; for Me, thy pains:

So, goest thou luminous upon thy way;
And where thou comest, lo, there is the day!
Dark places lightened see in thee My face,
And haste within the radiance lit by grace!

LI

"CONSIDER THE FOWLS OF THE AIR"

AND more the Master spake:—
                              "Poor foolish ones,
Ye gather trivial treasures, serve false gods,
And all because upon yourselves ye take
The care belongs to Me—why, Father, else?
Wherefore, I say, let never anxious thought
For your life's maintenance in that due place,
Wherein ye find yourselves, weigh on your heart:
Why fret with petty cares for meat and drink,
For seemly raiment, what thou shalt put on?
Think of thy life itself—how great a thing
God gives thee and maintains from day to day!
Who gives thee very life, can give the rest,
And knows the daily needs of thee and thine;
With tenderness, and soft regard, provides
All needful, beautiful and seemly things
To garb, sustain, and gladden life He gives!
See ye the birds—how gay and free are they!
No anxious care disturbs their happy mood—
Where shall they shelter? How shall they get food?
They sow not, reap not, gather not in barns,
And yet their heavenly father feedeth them:
Think, are ye not much more worth than they?
Then do ye, like the fowls, go blithe and gay;
As men, provide; but pray with open beak,
Your God shall fill, e'en while the words ye speak."

LII

"Consider the Lilies of the Field"

FOOLISH, thou thinkest, thou directest all;
But who by anxious thought can make himself
Taller, by inch, than God through Nature left?
If figure, face, the colour of thine hair,
Be not for thy determining, be sure,
All that maintains thy life, the Father's care!
Would'st in fair garb adorn the common ways,
Go beautifully in thine house and street,
And thinkest, God knows not of this need of thine?
He keeps ten thousand spinners all the day
In eager labour for thy fair array:
For thee the Tyrian dye, the jewel rare,
Hath secreted, that thou their glories, share.
Loves He not beauty, grace, and texture fine?
Nay, see the lilies, how they radiant shine!
What tincture can produce so fine a hue
As wear these blossoms, crimson, purple, blue,
That under foot ye tread the while I speak?
Not Solomon, I say, I, who have seen,
Could ever clothe him in such lustrous sheen!
And yet the flowers toil not, nor spin, nor fret!
Before their Maker grow they where they stand;
Beauty and sustenance draw from His hand:
Joy of a day, the grass, cut down and burned,—
Yet of your Father cherished while it lasts;
Say, are not ye, then, worthier of His care?
So be not anxious, what to eat or drink,
Wherewith to clothe yourselves, where shelter get,
Be ye as children, seek your meat from God;
Your Father knoweth that ye need these things.
Nothing is yours to lack, so seek ye first
Your Father's kingdom, and His righteousness;

These are for them who seek; and whoso find,
All other things are added in due kind;
So, children, be not careful for the morrow;
To-morrow bringeth its own cause of sorrow
But day by day go on, and trust in God.

LIII

"ASK AND YE SHALL RECEIVE"

THE Master said:—
But ye must ask, my children; all is yours,
But not a careless boon your God confers:
Who asketh not, is not aware of need,
Would waste that good he getteth without heed.

But he who finds void places in his life,
A hundred needs, distresses, painful strife,
He looks about for help, and sure supply
All hungers of his heart to satisfy;

Then lifts his eyes to God who giveth all;
And on his Father he makes haste to call;
Behold, God, watching tender o'er his days,
Hears him and answers even while he prays!

LIV

"SEEK AND YE SHALL FIND"

"WHO wants not more than things of touch and sight,
How should he in the Father's gifts delight?
But turns he, surfeited, from common joys
Aware of craving all his days annoys,—
He sets himself to seek what shall appease,
And, till he solve life's riddle, finds no ease:
Lo, this man, seeking, shall to God be led,
And find in Him wherewith his soul is fed."

LV

"Knock and it shall be opened"

MEN spend their days in knocking at closed doors,
Which, opened, offer nothing but bare floors
They tread towards other limitations yet;
And, good they ask of life, they fail to get.

There is a door where no man knocks in vain;
The feeblest rapping gettest answer plain;
"Come in," a Voice; and lo, the door stands ope,—
Within, fulfilment of his utmost hope;
For there the Father, waiting for His child—
Come home at last from wanderings in the wild!

LVI

"ANY OF YOU BEING A FATHER"

"HOW doubt your father's love? So good are ye
That better than your God ye think to be?
Thy child asks bread—quick, grantest thou his wish,
Nor giv'st a serpent when he asks a fish:
Is't only thou who hast a fathers heart?
Thou, thou alone, who know'st a fathers part?
That very tenderness, I gave to thee
That thou, the little ones, bring up for Me:
Thou, too, a child, wilt thou not know Me kind,
Waiting to grant according to thy mind
If thou, what I may give, wilt duteous ask,
Nor with thy wilful cries My Father task?
That child who stone or serpent asks for meat,
Unnatural father, he, would let him eat!"

Dedication of the Western Portal

NOW, having laid due shapen stone upon stone,
(This, writ with precept plain, and that, with tale,
On these, surpassing poems of the world),
And built that Western Portal, narrow way,—
Then spake the Lord: "Take heed how ye shall tread
That portal, which excludes inflated pride,
And heavy-laden greed, and lingering lust;
Which lets in only love, of eager step,—
Treading the entrance court with ready feet
So it may reach the greater things beyond,
The body of the Church, where God is all."—
This portal having builded for His Church
On the first day of founding:—"Take ye heed,"
Saith Christ, our Founder, "that ye enter in:
For every man goes searching for a way
To lead him to fulfilment: on every side
Are broad and open roads which promise ease,
And that imagined thing a man hath not,
And must have for completion.
Down this or that broad road, of pilgrims full:
But, what the end of all this sedulous zeal,
Or, easy-going pleasure in the path?
Who journey takes, except to destination
His steps would reach? But these go on their way,
Nor ask themselves the end. Yet, every day,
Approach they closer to the verge of that abyss
Where lost souls sink who have not come to God.
There is none other final goal for men
Save the Kingdom of God Who made them for Himself;
And he who heedless takes some easy path,
That leads not to the kingdom, what for him?
His hopes, desires, ambitions, ways of thought,

His wealth, his pleasures, lusts, indulgences—
All of them things that perish in the using!
What then survives of all he made himself?
Of all the toys he got to please himself?
The man has won his goal—and perisheth!

"See then ye enter through this narrow porch
To-day I have constructed in your sight:
Only meek, sweet submissive souls find room,—
The pitiful and peaceable and sad,
For sins of all men and their own; and these
Must labour, love and learn, and pray alway!"
The wistful Passion in the Master's tones
Moved every heart; and lo, they all gat up
(In purpose), pressing to the narrow Way
A multitude moved as a single man!
What is within the Portal, they shall know
Who follow on to know the Lord; but now,—
Eye hath not seen, nor heart of man conceived
The riches of that Church the Lord had founded.

LVIII

AUTHORITY OF THE MASTER

THE Master having ended all His speech,
The people stood and pondered: in a while,
Low talk went round; Church, in the thought of Christ
Had no dim outline in their minds: the way,
The narrow way by which to enter in,—
What is it? vaguely asked they. This one thing
They knew; *their Master* spake, and Him they heard;
(Ah, happy men who heard their Master's call!)
Authority perceived they; named it right;
Scarce knowing what He bade—that would they do:
And each, fervent of aspect, looked on each
As on him the Lord had bidden! Holy day,
When a man receives that call he must obey!
And as they spake together, knowing Him,
The Master who should bid them evermore,—
Bethought one here and there of other times
When His authority was manifest,—
This Lord of lords, life's issues could control,
And summon health to sick boy far away;
And bid disease retreat and devils flee;
The inmost counsels of High God reveal;
Forgive men's sins, and heal them! Who is this,
But very Christ of God! Master and Lord!

(Ah, Christ, full weary go we, seeking place
    Where One doth bid, and we must needs obey!
Show us—as showd'st Thou these—*our Master's* face,
    And bid us go and serve Him every day!)

INDEX

OF SUBJECTS AND REFERENCES TO PASSAGES IN THE HOLY
SCRIPTURES ON WHICH EACH OF THE POEMS IS FOUNDED.

BOOK I

AUTHORITY

(MANIFESTED AND RECOGNIZED)

"HE IS LORD OF All"

I

Christ heals the Nobleman's son   15
St. John 4:43-54

II

Christ preaches at Nazareth and is Rejected   18
St. Luke 4:14-30; St. Matthew 4:12; St. Mark 1:14;
Isaiah 61:1, 2; 1 Kings 17:9; 2 Kings 5:14

III

Christ teaches in Galilee   22
St. Matthew 4:13-17; St. Mark 1:14, 15; Isaiah 9:1, 2

IV

Call of the Four Fishers   23
St. Mark 1:16-20

V

Authority of the Lord: the Demoniac Delivered   25
St. Mark 1:21-28; St. Luke 4:31-37

VI

Peter's Wife's Mother healed   29
St. Mark 1:29-31; St. Luke 4:38, 39; St. Matthew 8:14, 15

VII

"At Even ere the sun was set"   31

St. Mark 1:32-34; St. Luke 4:40, 41; St. Matthew 8:16, 17

VIII

Jesus prays in the Desert   33

St. Mark 1:35; St. Luke 4:42

IX

In Galilee   35

St Mark 1:36-39; St. Luke 4:42,43, 44; St. Matthew 4:23-25

X

The Fisher's Net   37

St. Luke 5:1-11

XI

The Leper healed   40

St. Mark 1:40-45; St. Luke 5:12-16; St. Matthew 8:2-4

XII

Jesus heals the Man with the Palsy   43

St. Mark 2:1-12; St. Luke 5:17-26; St. Matthew 9:1-8

XIII

The Call of Levi   47

St. Mark 2:13-17; St. Luke 5:27-32; St. Matthew 9:9-13; Micah 6.6

XIV

The Jews are rejected   51

St. Mark 2:18-22; St. Luke 5:33-39; St. Matthew 9:14-17

BOOK II

AUTHORITY
(VINDICATED AND DEFINED)

XV
The Man healed at Bethesda   57
St. John 5:1-16

XVI
Christ's Defence   61
1. The Oneness of the Father and the Son
St. John 5:17-21

XVII
Christ's Defence   65
2. Or Judgement committed to the Son
St. John 5:22, 23

XVIII
Christ's Defence   68
3. Of life
St. John 5:24-27

XIX
The World to Come (The Disciple)   70
St. John 5:29

XX
Christ's Defence   74
4. The Witnesses: Condemnation of the Jews
St. John 5:30-47

XXI
Jesus walks in the Cornfields   78
St. Matthew 12:1-8; St. Mark 2:23-28; St. Luke 6.1-5;
1 Samuel 21:3-6; Numbers 28:9; Hosea 6:6

XXII
Law (The Disciple)   81
1 Samuel 21:3-8

XXIII
Christ restores the withered Hand   85
St. Luke 6:6-11; St. Mark 3:1-6; St. Matthew 12:9-14

XXIV
"He shall not strive nor cry"   88
St. Mark 3:7-12; St. Matthew 12:15-21; Isaiah 42:1-4

XXV
Unrest (The Disciple)   90

XXVI
Rest (The Disciple)   91
Isaiah 42:2

BOOK III

THE CHURCH
(FOUNDATIONS AND INSTITUTIONS)

XXVII
The Church of Christ   95
St. Luke 6:12: St. Mark 3:13

XXVIII
The calling of the Twelve   99
St. Luke 6:13-16; St. Mark 3:14-19

XXIX
The Ordination Charge   103
St. Luke 6:17-19

XXX
Blessed are ye poor   105
St. Luke 6:20

XXXI
Blessed are ye that hunger and thirst   106
St. Luke 6:21

XXXII
Blessed are ye that mourn   108
St. Luke 6:21

XXXIII
Of Persecutions   110
St. Luke 6:22-26

XXXIV
Order of the Day   112
St. Matthew 5:13-20

XXXV
Further Orders   114
St. Luke 6:27-38

XXXVI
The Nursery (the Disciple)   117

XXXVII
Six Parables   119
St. Luke 6:39-49

XXXVIII
The Sermon on the Mount   122
St. Matthew 5:1-12

XXXIX
At School (The Disciple)   123

XL
The old Rule and the New: Of Love and Hate   125
St. Matthew 5:21-26

XLI
Of Chastity   127
St. Matthew 5:27-32

XLII
Of Guarded Speech   129
St. Matthew 5:34-37

XLIII
"Be ye perfect   131
St. Matthew 5:38-48

XLIV
Of Alms   133
St. Matthew 6:1-4

XLV
Of Prayer   134
St. Matthew 6:5-8

XLVI
"Our Father"   136
St. Matthew 6:9-15

XLVII
Of Fasting   138
St. Matthew 6:16-18

XLVIII
Of being anxious   139
St. Matthew 6:19-21

XLIX
Of the Single Eye   140
St. Matthew 6:22,23

L
Of servng God and Mammon   141
St. Matthew 6:24

LI
"Consider the fowls of the air"   142
St. Matthew 6:25, 26

LII
"Consider the lilies of the field"   143
St. Matthew 6:27-34

LIII
"Ask and ye shall receive"   145
St. Matthew 7:7, 8

LIV
"Seek and ye shall find"   146
St. Matthew 7:7, 8

LV
"Knock and it shall be opened"   147
St. Matthew 7:7, 8

LVI
"Any of you being a Father"   148
St. Matthew 7:9-12

LVII
Dedication of the Western portal   149
St. Matthew 7:13-14

LVIII
Authority of the Master   151
St. Matthew 7:28-29

Made in the USA
Columbia, SC
19 August 2023